The Cabin
Away from it All

Other books by C. W. Gusewelle

A Paris Notebook

An Africa Notebook

Quick as Shadows Passing

Far from Any Coast

A Great Current Running: The Lena River Expedition

The Rufus Chronicle: Another Autumn

A Buick in the Kitchen

On the Way to Other Country

Another Cat at the Door

A Little Christmas Music

A Gift of Wings (with Charles Porter)

The Cabin
Away from it All

By C.W. Gusewelle

KANSAS CITY STAR BOOKS

STAR
BOOKS

"The Cabin: Away from it All"

by C.W Gusewelle

First Edition

Library of Congress Catalog Card Number: 2008939155

ISBN 978-1-933466-88-0

Edited by Katie Ingels Gusewelle and Les Weatherford
Book Design by Vicky Frenkel
Illustrations by Eric Craven

Printed in the United States by Walsworth Publishing, Marceline, Missouri.

Published by Kansas City Star Books, 1729 Grand Blvd., Kansas City, Mo. 64108.

To order copies, call StarInfo at 816-234-4636 and say "Books."

Order on-line at www.TheKansasCityStore.com.

STAR
BOOKS

Dedication

To my parents, Hugh and Dorothy,
and to their granddaughters,
my daughters,
Anne and Jennie

Spring

1

In the half-light of the waking hour, the thermometer on the cabin porch stands just two degrees above 50. I've started a little fire in the iron stove – just enough to chase the early chill. My wife and daughter still are sleeping. The dogs have been fed. And there's time now to sit in the magical stillness and relish the gift of such a day. No finer morning of middle spring could be imagined.

The whippoorwills have been chorusing, each three-note whistle preceded by a click. But now, as if on command, they go silent all together. From valleys to the south and west the owls start up, hoo-hoooo-ing the declarations of their territory. The squirrel, an irritable riser, begins a metallic scolding from his branch above the wood pile. Beneath the porch eave, the crested flycatcher is on her nest, while her mate goes prospecting for a seed.

The western sky still is full of night, but then it lightens to a rich, uninterrupted blue. An early crow, a solitary, cuts an arc across it. The woods that wrap the cabin clearing are a massed and solid presence, but soon the mounded upper treetops are defined against a paler wash.

And the day is begun.

A whisper of a morning breeze stirs. Carried on the river of the air is the far-off bark of a dog. Then the growl of a balky engine being turned. Then the clatter of a house door that cannot be nearer than a quarter-mile. Then the engine again, this time catching. The breeze freshens, and in it the treetops move like dancers. The sound of their dancing shuts out the rest, and the world is drawn down again to the perimeter of the clearing: the pine trees we planted, the irises that seldom bloom, the plum tree that never bore, the place where a vegetable garden used to be.

Presently a stirring can be heard in the cabin's back room. I fill the kettle and set it heating for coffee. My ladies appear, and we take our breakfast on the porch. Then, loading the dogs, we drive around to the gate that leads into the big fields and along the rutted lane to the crest of the land, a half-mile from the danger of any road.

There we let the pups, Pete and Bear and Cyrus, have their run. It is hard for them to be bounded by a fenced yard in the city. It's better than the confinement some creatures endure, but hard nonetheless. They're in their prime and, although not winged, they long to fly like hawks. So for them these country adventures are important.

From the rise where we stand beside the car, the view is clear in every direction.

To the north lies the steep wooded valley that I've long imagined would be an ideal site for the building of a lake. On high ground to the east of that is a hay field in which deer often are seen, and farther on, beyond it, is a stretch of forest we call "the wilderness." Two friends lost themselves there once while hunting, and came out finally more than a mile away behind another man's house. Due west there's another pasture, bounded by dark woods on three sides. And south of that is the cabin, past the remnant of an old fence row in which a stack of fieldstones marks the burial place of a good dog – sire of two of the present ones, grandsire of the other.

All of that can be seen from here, and to every inch of it some memory – painful or sweet – attaches.

The dogs make several grand excursions almost to the end of seeing, visible only as momentary flashes of orange and brown and white through the sea of grass. The air begins to warm and they turn back, having had the freedom they needed, wanting water, now, and shade.

There's a pond in a corner of that field that, although rich with fish, tends often to be whipped by wind. This midday, however, it lies still as glass. My daughter and I put in the boat, and spend an hour casting flies to the edge of the reeds. Mostly the fish we catch there are put back to grow and give sport another day – so many times released that my wife says each of them must be named. This time, though, we keep just enough for lunch for the three of us.

There is no better fare than filets of bluegill barely an hour out of the water, eaten at a porch table in the open air on a splendid spring day. It's of such small, utterly commonplace events as these that perfect days are made. And it is the collected memories of such days that fill and complete a life, especially if one is lucky enough to share them with ones you love.

2

I was a young man away serving in the Army when my parents, whose names were Hugh and Dorothy, told me in a letter what they'd done. That scrap of Ozark land was the single capricious big investment of their whole lives – lives pinched to caution, as so many were, by memory of the Great Depression.

Forty scrub-timbered acres at a road corner not far from the Osage River . . . a rough one-room shack of native oak boards sawed somewhere in the hills nearby and nailed up green . . . a pond that was hardly more than a mud hole – that's all there was. Fifteen hundred dollars they'd paid for the place, and their recklessness must have frightened them a little.

The man they bought it from had built the shack

himself, hastily, while the unseasoned oak still would accept a nail. He'd covered over the outside with a patchwork of many-colored asphalt shingles scavenged from roofing jobs in town, and then entertained himself by lying on his cot inside, drinking whisky from the bottle and loosing pistol shots at mice – real ones, or creatures from his delirium – that dodged among the roof planks. The inner ceiling was pocked by his fusillades. Outside, the bottles he had emptied glittered where he'd flung them into the weeds.

Hugh and Dorothy gathered up the bottles and trash, and paid someone to haul them off. They found a man with a bulldozer, and hired him to spend a half-day raising the earthen dam, so that the mud hole became a respectable if smallish pond, which they stocked with fingerling game fish. They planted redbud and dogwood trees beside the cabin. By repeated journeys over it with a push mower, Hugh beat the weedy clearing down into something nearer a lawn. On trees along the road, as a rite of ownership, they tacked up signs forbidding trespass. All this their happy letters told.

One day, they wrote, they were having a picnic

on the freshly mown lawn and noticed a gaunt old man squatting on his haunches at the gate out by the gravel lane. Hugh went down to ask what he wanted. The fellow wore ragged clothes and a mean look. He was there, he said, about those trespass signs. He didn't like them. He'd freely used that land, had swum his horses in the pond when it pleased him to, for a good deal longer than they'd owned it. He didn't like being told where he could go and where he couldn't.

Fires burned across the country regularly, he declared, and spat. Neighbors looked out for neighbors. But any man forbidden entry would gladly let a cabin burn!

The old man wasn't a neighbor at all, Hugh discovered later. He was only the malicious patriarch of an evil-spirited clan – a whole tribe of truants who, between intermittent floodings, camped in doorless houses, sharing the houses with chickens and sharp-backed hogs, in a derelict hamlet beside the river several miles away. Passing afoot on some errand of likely mischief, he had seen the signs. And they had fanned the coals of his everlasting hatred of men unlike himself, with their concept of property.

The next year I came home from soldiering, took a newspaper job. And the summer after that, helped build a screened porch onto the front of the cabin. We spent most of a week at that, Hugh and I, swearing sometimes at each other but mostly at our shared ineptitude with tools. And in the end were immoderately pleased with our work, however botched and out of square it might have been.

3

Years passed. The cabin was broken into twice by thieves, but never set afire. The minnows in the pond grew to be serious fish. The dogwoods and redbuds reached their age for flowering.

In one of those years – because I had read the writers of the generation before mine and supposed it was a young man's obligation to do it, I left newspapering to spend several months sleeping in the orchards, olive groves and threadbare pensions of France, Italy and Spain. I came home from that adventure all but penniless, with no job, but determined work at learning the writing craft.

So I drove a cab for a month, managed to save $76, and with that meager grubstake, with autumn coming on, borrowed the cabin for a winter's living. It wasn't used in that season anyhow.

The lane toward which my cabin fronted was gravel then, and the old cars and broken trucks passing slowly along it raised rooster tails of chalky dust. On its far side, where there was only forest, there's a house now. Today the lane is traveled by youngsters in pickups, farmers on tractors and city folks on outings to view us rustics.

Two beagle pups came to me, foundlings, out of the frozen woods of that lonely winter. I later found their mother beside the road two curves away, where she'd been struck by a car, scattering her youngsters all across that neighborhood, left to make their own way. We made a team. They brought rabbits to the gun, and we shared the nourishment that resulted.

One of them, the one I named Shorty, was outwardly quite phlegmatic and content. In his heart, though, he was insecure. He groaned when you scratched his stomach. The other, his brother, was larger and more able and yet, somehow, never quite healthy. A case of distemper left him uncertain on trail, where once he'd been unfailing. But the hound's passion still was in him. And in later years, asleep on the rug at the foot of my bed, he would run and yelp in his dreams. I liked to imagine sometimes what country he was seeing, and wonder whether he would ever see it again. That one's name was Slatz.

We spent the next 14 years together, those little hounds and I. As with any friends, it hurts very much still to think of them gone. I suppose in all that time I spoke more words to them than to anyone alive except my blood family. They died just months apart, and I buried them side by side on a piece of ground that, as pups, we used to run together – on the hillside sloping down to the pond. The scene of many triumphs.

One spring day years later, out walking, I came across the place again. Not quite by accident. Nothing ever is entirely by accident. Moss of the woodland floor had crept up to cover the two piles of stones. The trees were budded, the birdfoot violets just coming. I couldn't tell you how many exact such days those two and I had spent in that woods together.

One wall of the room where I sometimes write, where I'm writing now, is covered entirely with photographs. There's one of a man I once worked for, and in whose home I spent many hours of boyhood. Gone now. Another is a scene from some battlefield of a generation ago, with Russian women bending over their dead in the rain and mud. Yet another of a white-haired poet in Topeka, Kansas, reading from his manuscript beside a window sometime in the 1960s, on one of the last afternoons of his life. Of a friend in a duck blind, also gone – the blind and the man both. Of other friends, met since in foreign countries, and still others moved away to distant states. Of my own daughters in their childhood years.

Shorty and Slatz are there in one of the photographs, side by side in a brushy covert. Their heads are raised, their eyes fixed off alertly at some distant point from which a sound has come. They are very young and very eager. They know that life is sweet, and they believe that there is nothing beyond that moment. That is how I look, too, in the pictures on that wall. It is how all of us look – all of us arrested in time by the camera many years ago.

For a hound, today is an eternity. Maybe, like them, we would do better never to consider the shortness of the race.

4

As I remember that cabin winter now, across these nearly 50 years, I marvel at how the unhurried days seemed to fall neatly into segments – one part for cutting stove wood, one part for hunting squirrels and rabbits for the pot, another part spent at the typewriter, trying to learn better how to put one word after another.

About my only visitor during those months was an old man who also lived alone in a drafty ruin of a farmhouse two ridges away. He had a reputation for being hard, but for some reason we got on well. Sometimes I would split his firewood, and he would pay me in Mason jars of wild berries canned the year before. We would drink coffee, sitting close to the stove, and talk about the fish we would catch in the creek when spring came. Then spring did come, and one of his machines killed him.

Another friend of sorts was the strange, brooding and often stone-drunk fellow who kept the store I walked to four miles over the gravel for flour and shortening and other necessary grub. He was a great horseback quail hunter, when he could see to shoot. But his store burned, with his bird dogs under it, and broken-hearted that man died, too.

Between the days' obligations, there remained a lot of time for daydreaming and aimless wandering. Exploring out, I must have walked, in that winter, several hundred miles in all across frost-burned fields, through empty woods, past leaning barns and deserted houses, bleached silver and staring blankly from glassless window sockets.

Actually, of all that land I covered, the part that I cared for most – except for the cabin acreage itself – was a small, steep hollow I called the Fern Valley that adjoined it immediately to the north. Second-growth white oak trees, well-spaced and straight, grew on the valley's sides and gave home to plenti-ful squirrels, each squirrel a supper. An intermittent stream running down out of a wild pasture above tumbled over the polished lip of a limestone ledge, fell a dozen feet to carve a pool, then meandered on between mossy banks and, in season, a knee-high jungle of wild ferns.

If a man ever had some money, I told myself, he'd be a fool not to try to buy a place like that. I found out who the owners were, and even wrote them a letter telling of my interest. They wrote back, brusquely I thought, that their valley wasn't for sale. In any case, it was part of a larger tract of 400 acres which, if ever sold, they'd not want to divide. Evidently, though, they saved my letter.

Skip forward a few more years.

I'd gone back, finally, to the newspaper. I'd met and loved a woman. On a raw March weekend, with city friends helping, we planted several thousand pine seedlings in the cabin woods. And after the friends left, she and I together, hands aching with cold, set out 200 dogwoods along the road front-age. The next month, in April, we were married. That spring's wildfires took half the pines. In sum-mer, the rural electric cooperative sprayed its right of way. The wind-drift of herbicide killed all the dogwoods but three. And the following spring the letter came. Those people would sell the place, after all – but not the valley separately. The whole of it, 400 acres or nothing. And so it happened that on a pretty afternoon I sat with my wife of a year on a boulder in the cool shadow of the valley of ferns, with water rushing cheerfully over stones and around bends, and asked her leave to do an entirely illogical things.

The price was reasonable. That is, it was possible at least to imagine that someday the place might be paid for. The people whose land it was had had dreams of their own, but dreams and their health failed them. *Time had run out*, they wrote – a concept not easily understood until it happens – and they had to let it go. A sale contract was signed. In the week between then and the closing, timber thieves with saws and trucks savaged the woods, felling every tree of size, leaving a litter of raw stumps and wilting crowns. Or maybe it wasn't thieves.

"Take it or leave it," the owners' lawyers said at the closing. So maybe they'd arranged that treachery. I never could find out. They're dead, and it doesn't matter now.

5

The worst people in that country are animated by a feckless wickedness that can take the breath. But their numbers are mercifully few.

The best of the people in those hills, on the other hand, are so kind, so unfailingly gentle, so generous with their loyalty, their affection, and their few material goods that it seems quite inconceivable that they all sprang from the same stock and were shaped by the same experiences, though plainly enough it's true.

With more land had come new possibilities, and new concerns.

Like all the other untenanted farms, mine once had been home to someone. The Ginter Place it continued to be called, though any Ginters had long ago departed. Some time past, the barn had burned, but the house remained, or what had been the house – porch fallen, roof open to animals and sky, camped in freely by passers-by on foot. Only by a miracle was anything left at all.

John and Oma, the man and woman who came to live there, who made the house tight from weather and having saved it filled it with their lives, were of the second and wonderful kind. We fenced some fields, John and a neighbor and I, to rent for pasturage. Then someone set a fire out by the road, and the just-greening pasture burned to a desert of sifting ash. The next spring the field grew back. We bought a machine to pull behind our ancient tractor and harvest grass seed. First the machine broke. Then the tractor broke. The price for a pound of grass seed fell to less than a nickel – and *do you know* how much small seed it takes to make a pound?

It wasn't enough just to let the land lie idle, as it had lain for a generation. My father, Hugh, was country born. He had lived nearly his whole life in the city, but kept somehow a farmer's passion for the fruitful destiny of land. It wasn't right, he argued, for anyone to own a parcel of the earth and not cause it to produce. To produce *something*. So (not blaming him; I did it gladly and of my own volition) I bought from a neighbor six heifer calves and, not yet knowing it, further committed myself to my own destruction.

After that I sat more often at John and Oma's table. I loved them as dearly as one could love a brother and sister, neither of which I ever had. But too soon that man died. And his wife, wounded by all the memories that pressed upon her (even if they were good ones) left to live in a town nearby.

For a while after that, our experience with tenants was miserable. One oaf, three months behind on his rent, met me in the yard with a pistol, and declared, "You'll never get me out of here." But with the sheriff's help I did. The one after him pulled a mile of steel posts out of my fences, loaded them on a wagon, and took my posts and my wagon to Texas. He was succeeded by a young couple who'd lost their house in a winter fire. We let them move in, rent-free, until they could get their lives together. That spring I found them growing 50 marijuana plants in pots on the side porch.

But finally, it seemed our luck had turned. A new man came with his family to manage the place, and for almost three years it was wonderful again. My herd increased. The old farmhouse was made finer, redone from roof down at a cost of more thousands than we've ever spent improving any house in which we ourselves have lived. My wages hesitated only briefly in the checking account before passing through and on to make some further, never final, contribution to rural elegance.

But then . . . a worse catastrophe. Our new hired man and manager – no, this *friend*, this *collaborator* – gave in to his heretofore hidden curse, the disease of drink, and turned from a wonder of power and energy into a pathetic, mewling husk who stumbled crazed through the woods, cradling his bottle and, like some shot animal, bedding in the leaves wherever he happened to fall.

The spring before, down the path behind the cabin, I'd built a tree house for my two small daughters – a stilt house, actually, up among the trees – on the hillside looking down upon the little cabin pond. I liked to think of the pleasure they would have sleeping there, which they did at least once, or possibly twice.

But for a long time after that broken man left, for the greater part of a year, I went to the farm alone, never with my family. My two little hounds were under their cairns next to a rabbit trail. The paths in my woods were unwalked. The fish in the pond swam unmolested. I wore out two automobiles driving the 100 miles of highway from the city to that corner, but it wasn't ever a trip made in happy expectation. Only multiplying problems brought me now.

The young man who'd sat with his wife beside a stream in the valley of ferns all those years ago could not have been me. Nor could he, in his fatuous hunger for it, have been dreaming about any piece of land I know.

6

Somewhere in all this the government took an interest in my impoverishment. Only the mind of a bureaucrat would suspect that a taxpayer of modest means had, deliberately and for some hidden reason, contrived his own near ruin.

The audit lasted three months, required hundreds of hours of solitary work sorting and matching ledger entries, invoices and canceled checks. There were many trips to the Internal Revenue Service offices, carrying cardboard boxes of these assembled sortings. The auditor assigned to my case was a sweet and patient woman, a city woman, who as far as I could tell had never set foot on a farm and did not know a horse from a Hereford. Her expertise had to do with numbers, not woe. She just tapped into her adding machine figures from those boxes of papers I brought, then asked new questions, waiting for me to bring more boxes.

In the end, all the columns of numbers matched. It was demonstrated that I had not ruined myself for gain. But there remained, in the mind of the IRS, the possibility that the farm was a hobby and an amusement – in other words, that I had ruined myself for *pleasure*. To lay this last suspicion to rest, I was invited to submit an informal statement amounting to a kind of recapitulation or chronology of my involvement on the land.

I sat down to begin . . .

Broken machinery. Broken men. Bulls gone lame while breeding. Money-eating tenant houses. Fields of hay, mown but unbaled and rotting. Flash floods. Fires. Barren cows. Four-cent-a-pound grass seed. Rust in the wheat. Morning glories in the soybeans. Droughts that opened fissures underfoot. Threatened violence. Betrayal and disappointment without end.

I put it all on paper, in rich detail and burdened throughout with numbers. It is a queer experience to write a summary of nearly a third of your life to date, and to watch as it unfolds into a fool's tale. The story of Job pales alongside the compendium of tribulations I set down, all of them perfectly true. When it was finished, we howled with laughter my wife and I – the laughter of hysteria and heartbreak.

The brief statement I'd been asked to prepare ran to more than 15 typewritten pages, single-spaced. And after they had read it, with what must have been pity and amazement, the auditors closed the book on my defeats.

And yet, for all of that, I love the place still – especially that part of it I began with: the little acreage on the road corner; the cabin, improved and enlarged a bit over the years; and down the path behind it the small pond, surrounded by woods and bordered by the few of all those thousands of pine seedlings that managed to survive to be trees.

I spend time there as often as I can, even if I must go mostly alone now; even if my daughters have grown to women, and the idea of a night spent curled on hard bunks in the tree house no longer figures in their plans. For even with the place so haunted by hound shadows and people shadows and the strangely mocking memories of a younger and less complicated time, the cabin is still a place in the heart.

You hear men speak sometimes of taming the land. But that land of stones and bristling oaks and saffron-colored grasses is fearfully powerful. And it is fast forgetting. One spring night I heard there were more than 90 wildfires burning in the county. Some year, one of those will come sweeping un-resisted to obliterate every trace of anything I've touched.

Fire only does time's work, but does it faster.

7

The common wood tick (also called the hard tick, the dog tick and, less often, *Dermacentor variabilis*) is not an elegant creature.

But he is durable. You will have to give him that. Each spring for well over a century, the settlers of our southern forest have been burning the wood-lands in persistent faith that it will kill the ticks. The wildfires rage. Houses burn. Horses go mad. Valuable timber stands are scarred and destroyed. Wildlife is driven out. But spend several hours marching on foot across that smoking wasteland and you will come back clung over by ticks.

In the stretch of hills I know best, the stream courses and early wagon roads are dotted with the stone footings of vanished dwellings. Some of these homesteads, it may safely be supposed, were consumed by fires set to kill the ticks. Habitation has thinned. And still there are ticks - in multiples of multiples of human numbers.

I have read that the tick has been known to live

three years without food or drink. I take my hat off not only to the tick but to whichever scientist it was whose patience and constant observation we have to thank for that astounding piece of information. Can you imagine the resourcefulness, the sheer *chutzpah* it would take to secure a federal grant to spend three years watching a tick do nothing?

Perhaps more amazing even than the tick's ability to withstand hunger and thirst is the reaction this insignificant creature is able to arouse in soft-skinned city people meeting it for the first time. Upon discovering that the thing is on them, and, worse, that it is attached to them, the fact is made known in whispers.

The afflicted count it no consolation that this tick - their tick - may have waited three years for a drink. A transport of shame and revulsion overcomes them. They speak of their condition as one might discuss a social disease. Closely related persons of the same gender withdraw into the next room and lock the door. There is a long, speculative silence. Presently the door is unlocked and an emissary is dispatched.

"Angel Pie has a tick." This vouchsafed in a low voice, eyes averted, the face of the bearer of the news flushed with humiliation.

"Has she? Well, that's good. Ticks only go for warm-blooded animals, so it must mean that Angel Pie is hot-blooded."

"I'm serious. She has a tick. It's a small one."

"Yes. They all start small."

"What should I do? She's in a state."

"Pull it off."

The emissary is recalled for consultation. Then emerges again.

"She says she can't pull it off. It's in an embarrassing place."

"All right." Taking a step toward the closed door. "I'll do it for her."

"*No!* Wait a minute!"

Invariably, then, the tick is gotten off unaided.

Covering a tick with petroleum jelly is rumored to cause it to release its grip. A daub of nail polish is said also to be effective – the more expensive polishes, naturally, producing a superior result. Some advise holding a lighted match near the parasite, although, depending on location, the consequence of that can be tragic.

Country people, after a century of failed burning, have no faith in these measures. And I have spent enough time among them to adopt their casual attitude, which is that ticks, like morel mushrooms and wildflowers in bloom, are simply part of the natural order of the season. Some come off in the bath. Some you have to pull off. Most of the others, after enough time has passed and they have achieved sufficient size, sooner or later come out in the comb.

You would be surprised how the explanation of this reduces the congestion of weekend visitors at our cabin at the edge of the woods.

8

Journalism is a hasty art. If there were time, I would have liked to research extensively the question of toads, because I think, as with anything that lives and lusts and perishes, there must be a good deal about them worth knowing. What I have, instead, is only the product of an hour's casual observation.

We were beside a pond in one of the cow pastures, one daughter and I. The afternoon breeze had hushed. The evening was coming softly on. A few moments earlier, a family of a dozen geese had crested a woodline and passed low overhead on their way to the night's resting place. In the great stillness, the rush of their wingbeats could be clearly heard.

Together we watched the sun fall, and the sky across the field ripen with a blend of peach and darkest blue. It was a good time to be anywhere, especially with someone who's a friend.

Suddenly, from the far side of the pond, an electronic trill was heard. A moment later, from another quarter of the shore, an answer was hurled back. All around the perimeter, then, there rose a gathering choir, growing in number of voices, intensifying in shrillness. Until we were enveloped entirely in a din of creaking and screaming so vast that it seemed to fill the whole visible universe and resonate inside the head. Each voice was slightly different in tone. Each song distinct in its cadence or duration. Plainly, though, the singers were of the same race of creature.

Singling one voice out from the others, my daughter followed the racket to its source. Its author was a toad. A surprisingly small toad, an inch of him at most, grayish-brown on top, perched at the pond's edge. We knelt to see him better in the poor light, and he was undisturbed by our being there. He had other things to think about, and work to do.

As we bent close, he inflated his throat to perhaps half the size of his whole body, and then shot out a burst of sound that lasted 10 seconds or maybe 15. Unless we'd seen it, we'd never have believed a beast that small capable of so terrific a howl. If human beings could emit a cry of such dimension proportionate to our size, it would be a nightmare weapon able to blow down buildings and knock airplanes from the sky.

We watched him, amazed, through several repetitions of his feat, which he seemed to take pretty much for granted. And all around the little pond were dozens, or possibly hundreds, of other virtuosos like himself. I say *himself*, himself, although for all I know the singers may have been herselves. Or it could be that, with toads, both genders sing. You see, there's the handicap of never having time to look into things properly.

If I had to guess, I'd say their performance had something to do with the season of the year and the time of reproduction. Probably they were singing to charm another toad. But why would that be necessary, considering the great multitude of them around the pond and the fact that toads, in any case, have only other toads to go to?

On the other hand, if their songs were different, mightn't their purposes be different too? Maybe some of them were crying out cautionary arias about the raccoon that comes at night or the heron with his skewering beak. Maybe some were singing for the pure joy of being toads on such an evening.

Maybe some had been told they had nice voices.

We watched until it was too dark to see them any more, and we couldn't know.

But toads know.

9

Evidently the discussion of outhouses does not violate the canon of good taste, since *The New York Times* published a eulogy to them on the front page of a recent edition. Soon, according to the story, only snakes and wasps will be using the privy.

It may be true, as *The Times* said, that the fine old one- or two-holer is relied on today by a mere 0.64 percent of American households. But the reports of its demise have been greatly exaggerated. If you don't believe that, you can ask the hunting friends who come to my cabin in the woods when the primitive plumbing system, drained before the previous autumn's first hard freeze, has not yet been put back in service, and the only comfort to be found is at the end of a path behind my clearing.

Mine, if I may say so, is the Taj Mahal of outhouses.

Five or six of us invested a fair sum of money and most of a long weekend in its construction. When completed, it had nearly every amenity you could imagine: a mirror, a battery-powered overhead light, dustpan and whisk broom for housekeeping, and a magazine rack filled with – scandalous to say – *Playboy* magazines. Just for the record, the choice of reading matter wasn't mine. One of the hunters brought those magazines.

Time passed. The batteries in the light ran down. The mirror fell and broke. Mice chewed off the straws of the whisk broom and used them for nest building. The magazines were disfigured by having certain selected pages inexplicably torn out. A wildfire burning up through the woods from the road charred the back of the structure and burned off the roof. The damaged parts were cut away and replaced – the job done so cleverly by a man of the neighborhood that you'd never know it had passed through the flames.

The magazine rack survived, although its contents, regrettably, did not.

On the chance that the salaciousness of those publications may have been in some part to blame for the visitation by fire, I have restocked the rack with literature put out by the Department of Conservation, the Prairie Foundation, the Wild Turkey Federation and my wife's church. With a fresh coat of battleship gray paint, the privy was restored to its original magnificence, and it remains so today. Like a seasoned veteran of past campaigns, it stands ready to be summoned into service once more by the next freeze.

The splendor of my outhouse is no accident. I have childhood memories of other ones – memories that, when they come back to me at odd moments, could almost cause me to faint.

One was out behind the farmhouse to which

I was taken for visits in my childhood years. A grandmother lived there, my father's mother, and also an uncle, trying to wring a living from a tract of poor and steeply gullied land. The other was beside a lake in the far north of Minnesota, and was the common facility for several rough cottages. I loved that area – the fishing, the sharpness of the morning air, the beauty of the water and the woods. But always, at some point of every day – the beginning or the end of it – one had to face the horror of the outhouse.

My privy has nothing in common with those. Once, however, when friends came to see us at the cabin, the husband confided that since his wife's dread of a trip down the path was so great, and the nearest service station was on the highway 27 miles away, the duration of their visit would have to be limited.

And, indeed, they did not stay with us long, which was a pity. Because it's fresh as a spring daisy, my outhouse. That lady had nothing to fear but fear itself.

10

For as long as I've known that country neighborhood, people have spoken of the presence of the panther.

One man has seen it cross the night road in the lights of his pickup truck. Another found its pug marks printed clearly in the mud of the creek bed below his pasture. Another claimed to know its denning place, in the cellar of a certain long-abandoned house, though when I went there myself to investigate, no evidence of the creature – no hair, scat, or bones of a kill – could be detected.

It was, I years ago decided, a harmless country legend, like rumors of Indian burial places, hidden loot of Cole Younger's outlaw gang, and the "bottomless pit" that's said to be somewhere on my farm. Life is hard in that hill country. The terrain is steep, the fields stony and poor, the summers hot and often rainless. What fire and failure haven't ruined, the government has drowned under the man-made calamity of a muddy reservoir. Is there anyone alive, hemmed round by such misfortune, who would not welcome the presence – or even the idea – of something fabulous to lighten the burden of the known?

A cougar or mountain lion was, of course, the beast they spoke of, though "panther" is the name locally preferred, perhaps for the more mysterious resonance of the word. Last year, a farmer making hay on shares in one of my fields told of seeing it bound into the woodline ahead of his machine. But I gave no importance to the report. The panther was a fiction, or a figment of collective imagination. Of that much I was sure.

Until this spring – when I may have seen the thing.

I was standing with two friends, visitors from distant states, at the edge of that hay field the farmer had spoken of. From right to left at the field's far side, a tannish creature went loping across in the clear light of middle morning.

"See there, a coyote," said one of the friends, pointing..

The animal passed from view behind a plum thicket, and we were starting to turn away when, by purest chance, a second creature presented itself, trotting along the same far wood line.

"Another one," I said, only half-looking because I knew what it surely was.

"Wait a minute," said the other friend. "That's no coyote. It's too big, and the tail's wrong. Too long and smooth. It moves more like some kind of cat."

That from someone with no knowledge of the local legend, but with better eyes than mine, and familiar with the out-of-doors.

It's only an anecdote, not science. The sighting was across an open field, but for less than half a minute, without binoculars, at a distance of 200 yards. As testimony in court, it would be worthless. But the little episode has made a convert of me. The deer of our neighborhood have increased their numbers stupendously, and deer are the cougar's natural prey. So I tell it now as absolute fact to anyone who'll listen.

"There were three of us. We all saw it, and there's no doubt about it," I say, being careful to call it by its local name. "It was a panther for sure."

I've discovered what the local people always understood. It's fine to think there's still some magic to be met in a piece of country you imagined you knew so well.

11

In past years, the instrument I used in the hope of attracting wild turkeys was a box call, handmade from the wood of the hedge apple tree, the Osage Orange, a prized gift from a fellow hunter. I am adding to my arsenal now a new tool, a mouth call, which, according to the man on the instructional tape, is the deadliest ever devised – superior to tube calls, peg-and-slate calls, wing-bone calls or any other kind. Mastery of it, however, requires a certain investment of time before one can evoke from it the correct range of yelps, cackles, putts and clucks.

The important thing is learning to avoid the "gag

point." At least that's what the man on the record says. You begin by inserting between the tongue and the roof of the mouth a diaphragm apparatus resembling a primitive birth control device. That is where the gag point comes into play.

Hold the call too far forward in your mouth and you will get no noise at all out of it, or at best a pitiful squeak. Let it slip too far back and you will retch. Turkeys, the man says, have an uncritical ear. They will gobble in reply to an owl's hoot, a horn's honk or the bang of a car door closing. But they have not been known to respond to the sound of the hunter throwing up.

I tried practicing at home and my first efforts were predictably amateurish. I produced no yelps or clucks – only a kind of moist flatulence. My wife quickly reached the gag point, and she was not even using the call. So I brought the thing to the office and gave a cackle or two from my desk. Plainly something still was wrong with the tone. For, while there were some fellow turkeys – that is, journalists – well within earshot and several even in sight, none of them replied.

So I retired with my call to the men's restroom where, behind the locked door of one of the stalls, I could perfect my skills unselfconsciously. That place was wonderful for the purpose. It resonated like a concert hall. Whether or not I sounded any more like a turkey, the volume was astonishing. The outer door opened and two colleagues were heard to enter. I hit them with a series of hard, fast yelps.

"What the hell was that?" said one of them uneasily.

Now newspaper folk, in case you haven't noticed, like to believe they have an answer for everything. They abhor the phrase: I don't know. So the other one replied with complete authority.

"It's nothing," he said. "They're just adjusting one of the toilets."

"Yeah?" said the first one, much relieved. *"Well, they're really screwing that thing down tight!"*

It is now a little more than a week before the season opens, and I have made no detectable progress.

The gag still is a problem. I listen to those recorded sounds and have no more idea how they are produced than I had when I started. However, there is hope. A successful turkey hunt is said to depend only half or less on one's skill with a call. The rest is stealth, woodcraft and pure cleverness.

When you go into the bushes after turkeys, the man on the record advises, try to look as much as possible like a leaf. So that is where I am putting my chips now – on looking like a leaf. I concentrate on it in my spare time. With application, an odd feeling of leafiness has actually begun to take hold.

It is not easy. But it is quiet. And it has the further advantage of being something almost anyone can practice and keep his breakfast down.

12

In the last two days, friends began assembling for the annual ceremony we call our spring wild turkey hunt. Two have come from the West Coast, two more from Florida, one from New York and two from Kansas City. Others, including perhaps the Indiana pair, will arrive in the week ahead.

Today is Sunday, and this morning – almost at the end of April – it snowed. Only a few vagrant flurries, but enough to remind us that nature rarely takes our plans into account. Tomorrow, the season's first day, we'll strike forth at a pitch-black hour of morning to take our stations in the woods, listening to the melodic calls of whippoorwills, the hoots of barred owls and the annoyed replies of turkey gobblers.

That is, if the weather obliges, which sometimes it does not.

One year I began the hunt hunkered miserably under a poncho while thunder crashed, lightning rent the pre-dawn sky and hail the size of popcorn came rattling down. Another year, on the day before the opener, it snowed a *real* snow, an inch or so of heavy, wet flakes the size of quarters. On such a morning, when the clock radio emits its howl of country music at half past the hour of 4, it's somehow hard to remember what grudge it was you had against the turkey. And when wives later ask why it is that every spring must be organized around this curious enterprise, no answer readily comes to mind.

But here we are again, at this humble little cabin at the edge of the oak woods. And somehow it does feel right.

Rich memories surround us. The rush of years is halted and turned back by pictures on the cabin's walls. In several of those, one longtime member of our group, Gene Ayres, is alive again, his presence with us still. Near that is an informal snapshot of a teacher to whom I owe an unpayable debt for the luck of my working life. Gone several years now, that fine man. And in the hallway to the bunkroom there's a photo of my parents at the pond – the two of them much younger than I am now – my mother holding a wonderful big fish, my father smiling proudly behind her.

And tacked up on one wall is a good-humored reminder of mortality, whose author I don't know: *When I die,* it says, *I want to go quietly, in my sleep, the way my grandfather did – not screaming like the passengers in his car.*

I'm well aware that there are readers who will be mystified, or even repelled, by this account of a gang of friends, come together for the declared purpose of hunting turkeys. There was a lady out in Kansas who used to send me messages written in orange Crayola, signed only Ms. Sue, saying that if I didn't give up my vile hunting habit, she and her associates would be coming after me to injure me, or maybe even *take me out.*

But, for some of us, the hunt itself is the least part of the reason for our April gatherings. In any case, I have no intention of writing about my occasional successes. One wouldn't want to get crossways with as gentle-hearted a soul as that.

13

When you read this, if you bother to, probably it will be after a full night's untroubled rest. Your morning coffee will be fresh at hand, and breakfast will be cooking. Comfortable in robe and slippers, you will arrange yourself in a soft chair and fecklessly consider, dilettante that you are, *Do I want to read this man's effusions, or would I rather get on with something useful?*

I hate you.

At exactly that same moment, I already will have been awake several hours. Long before the first faint suggestion of a dawn, drugged with sleeplessness, I will have tripped over roots, gotten my face lashed by twigs, and arrived finally at my post, where I'm condemned to pass half the day sitting on sharp stones, shuddering at first in the early cold, later sweating and crept over by bugs. Probably it will be raining.

You may notice that this is stated in the speculative future tense. That's because I'm writing it in advance. Where I'm going no typewriters will be found. That's the one mercy of it all.

I try to remember how or why I ever got involved in hunting turkeys. But it's like trying to recall the very first time you succumbed to any vice that later came to rule you and ruin your life. The chronology of addiction gets muddled with time. It just happened. That's all I can say.

Now I find myself the annual host of this congregation of men and boys, who come to my cabin in the woods aflame with a passion to spill the blood of fowls. They are nice people, and friends all, but the idea of dead turkeys does not excite me as it used to. It's gotten to be something of a trial.

The main problem is that these nimrods do not appear all at once. They are busy folk. They have commitments – appointments scheduled, and balance sheets to be kept in the black. Things like school and business interfere. And I understand that. So some will have arrived this Sunday past, on the eve of the season's Monday opening. Their enthusiasm will be high. Stimulants will be taken, of the legal kind. The cabin will fill up with the racket of them displaying their skill with various kinds of turkey calls. Some of the calls will sound something like turkeys. Others will sound like ducks quacking or dogs barking.

"What time should we get up?" they'll ask each other.

"Four o'clock?"

"That's pretty late."

"Right. Better make it half-past three."

Even I am able to generate interest at the start. But that will have been Sunday. By the time you read this, the first shift of hunters will have gotten their birds, or not gotten them, and gone. The second shift will be in place. And the host of this affair, whose obligations are more or less continuous, still will be there – red of eye, nerves shot, trying manfully to pretend that these unending forays into the woods have some point.

The season lasts three weeks! You will never know, unless you've done it, how long three weeks can be.

Sometime tomorrow night the second shift will return to the city, to soft beds and dinner parties. And the first shift will come back for another try. Then that bunch will leave, and in the third and final week the mop-up crew will pull in from Indiana. Seeing them bound from their cars, dressed in camouflage suits, their eyes blazing, is the stuff of nightmares. I just take one day at a time, and try not to think ahead.

14

Wild dogs had been reported prowling in our country neighborhood. Two had been spied in my woods. I met that pair the other morning, just at dawn.

The first band of paler light had begun to show behind the trees on the ridge where I was sitting. The barred owls were hoo-hooing their announcement of another dampish day. Silent as shadows they came ghosting through the forest – a medium-sized yellow dog with pricked ears and a full, wolf-ish tail, and his partner who was all black, smooth-haired and slenderer.

"They ought to be shot," I'd heard people say. "They'll kill calves. They'd kill you if they could. Wild dogs are nothing to fool with."

No doubt it's sometimes true. Packs of them gone feral can be a terror. But two don't make a pack. And how, exactly, do you define a "wild" dog? Is it simply *any dog* that no caring hand has ever stroked, or one that someone mean has decided to stop feeding and has dumped or driven away? If so, does the blame lie with the dog or with the man?

I thought of that bitter winter so long ago when those two orphaned beagle pups came to make their nest under a log at the back of my clearing. Day and night I heard them trailing rabbits across the hills, trying to get by the only way they knew. Technically, I suppose, they were wild dogs, and might have been shot for that. Finally, though, they got the courage to venture close. I extended a hand, inviting them to approach, then touched first one and then the other. They came indoors. We shared our lives, until at last I had to lay them under two small piles of stone on the hillside where we first met, and where, when I pass there from time to time, the grief is as sharp as ever.

All this I was remembering as the yellow wolf-dog and his running mate came quartering toward me, where I sat in camouflage against a tree, face net on and gun across my lap. I made the soft call of a hen turkey, and they froze, not sure, quite, where the sound had come from. Then I made a little motion with my hand.

The yellow dog saw that. He wheeled round, gathered himself on his haunches, and rocked forward to begin his rush – all that in a single instant. Even in the poor light at 30 yards I could see how fierce and focused were his eyes. Then I reached up with my hand, lifted the net to show my face. And he stopped again, startled and confused to see a man where he'd thought a meal would be.

There's an old contract between my kind and his. Renegades on both sides sometimes break it, but he wasn't one of those. He may have been hungry, and without a door to go to. But he wasn't an outlaw. For a suspended moment we looked one another full in the face. Then he turned and went back the way he'd come, the black dog after him. He paused once, with a tree and a thin screen of brush between us, and turned to look back. Wondering, maybe, if I'd raised the gun.

I hadn't. The line that separates the ones who hunt to live from the ones who sleep warm on a rug is too fine, and drawn by circumstance. I had those two wild pups once. I don't shoot dogs.

15

One of the hunters came in with the news.

"There are two kittens under the cabin."

He'd seen their small faces in the moonlight, peering out from the opening to the crawl space beneath the floor, where in past years a variety of animals – a coyote, a stray dog, once a red fox vixen – had borne their litters. Just in a recent week, my wife had seen an armadillo scuttle into that convenient hideaway.

Kittens and armadillos, it seemed, might make a peculiar mix. But I telephoned a daughter, who would be arriving the next day and who is a dedicated capturer, socializer and adopter-out of strays.

"Bring food and cat carriers," I told her. I believed we could borrow a live trap from a friend who farms nearby. I don't know how it is that, most springs, some wild or homeless creature has found its way to that place for birthing. But it gives me pleasure to know the cabin gets used, even when I'm not there.

In the night, I could hear an intermittent scuttling and bumping under the wooden floor. And the following afternoon, the trap, the daughter, the cat carriers and the tins of tuna and other temptations arrived. The bait was put in place. Chairs were arranged in a half-circle in the yard, at a discreet distance from where the emergence was expected.

Time passed. A good deal of time. A timid nose appeared from the darkness. Then another.

I would not for the world embarrass the friend who'd reported the presence of kittens. He's experienced in the out-of-doors. His vision, with contact lenses, is quite normal. It had been night. The only light was the moon's. And except for being of different species, kittens and fox kits – in size at least – are not so unalike.

Gray foxes these were, not a month old, nine or 10 inches at most from their noses to the ends of their fat, furry little tails. And they moved in the uncertain, teetering manner of infants. More endearing wild youngsters hardly can be imagined – or more timid. Startled by some slight sound or movement, they would make a rush for the den but miss the hole and bump into the wall instead. But as long as we sat perfectly still, without speaking, they seemed hardly to be aware of their audience.

In time a third appeared. And another day, a fourth and a fifth.. We never saw the vixen, only her little ones. I suppose at night she went out to hunt, when they and we were sleeping. But during the days surely she was there nursing them in that dark space below the floor. For plainly they were well-nourished.

We decided, nonetheless, to supplement their rations a bit. Probably a true wildlife expert would disapprove of that intrusion on the natural order. But we did it for our own pleasure. The kits had refined tastes. For salad, they sampled the purple iris growing in a row along the cabin wall. As their main course, they preferred a cat food called Fancy

Feast, in particular the "gourmet chicken feast."

We spooned out dollops of the stuff on the ground outside the den. First one ventured out cautiously. Then another. Soon all were eating enthusiastically. As long as we remained motionless they hardly seemed to notice us. And with the passage of days, they became quite used to an audience.

As they grew larger and more robust, differences in temperament could be seen among them. One was the "alpha," a bit of a bully, and would bowl over any sibling that tried to poach a morsel. Another was noticeably the most timid. The cabin from time to time has trespassing mice. Two we caught in traps and deposited just outside the den. Within moments, they'd disappeared. The first real "kill."

Fox dens are often said to be foul-smelling, but there was no odor whatever to be detected, either inside the cabin or out. One night a cold front blew in, with howling wind, driving rain and temperature in the 30s. The next morning, we found the den entrance had been blocked with compacted leaves to keep out the wet and cold – the work of a wise and capable mother.

On a morning when two hunters we leaving, I had to rise at an unholy hour to see them off to the city to catch an early plane. Outside my window, in the soft shine of the yard light, I saw the four little ones romping like children, bouncing, wrestling, playing with leaves and twigs.

For most of three weeks we constituted a mixed family: the vixen, her five kits and we two-legged animals ranging in number from four to seven. Toward the end, the little foxes were taking cat food directly from the spoon. And at the final feeding on the last morning, one of them snatched the spoon from my hand and took it with him under the cabin. I told a friend about that afterward, and he said, wryly, quite correctly, that I'd been *outfoxed*.

I don't know if it ever happens that wild creatures ever return again to den in the place of their birthing.

But surely that cabin in a clearing of the Ozark woods will be among those kits' first memories, as it has been for my daughters. And I cannot help hoping that, in a later year, my girls and the foxes – or the progeny of some of them – will be there together to share the sweetness of another spring.

16

People acquainted with my addiction have asked how the turkey season went. I have not been asked about this a lot, you understand – the interest in turkeys being rather less universal than the abhorrence of hunting. But, yes, there has been an inquiry or two.

In fatigue and futility was how the season went.

We matched wits, the bird and I. Now, with my average-size brain of 1,400 cubic centimeters or maybe a bit less, I am back home. And the turkey, with his brain the size of an aspirin, is still out there uninjured in the woods. No doubt some naturalist with a nitpicking passion for accuracy will crawl out of the woodwork, complaining that the turkey's brain is not the size of an aspirin. It is the size of a pecan. Corrections will appear in all future editions of this book.

That is always the way of it. Turkeys ahead of writers every time. But has the naturalist ever personally autopsied one, or is he taking somebody's word for it? I say the bird's brain is the size of an aspirin, or maybe an Extra-Strength Tylenol. If I ever get close to a turkey, I have something else in mind than whipping out calipers to measure its cranium.

That is for a future spring, however. Just now I am recovering from the ordeal of this one.

This morning I came awake in a panic in the dark bedroom with a sense of having tragically overslept. I turned on the light and peered at the clock – which said 4:30 a.m. The season was over, but habit is a relentless master. And that is the dominant aspect of the hunt. The hunter is not allowed to rest.

The turkey has all the best of it. He goes to his roost when the sun declines, nods off immediately and sleeps 10 hours at a minimum, perfectly un-ruffled there on his branch, his dreams disturbed by nothing except an occasional happy recollection that tomorrow will be another day of the breeding season.

Meantime, the hunter is hunkered exhausted in some cabin or tent, practicing his calling technique and drinking stimulants to keep him awake while he discusses with his fellow assassins the strategy they will employ when – before they have gotten comfortable in their bedrolls – the trumpeting of the alarm sends them forth to battle again.

Several days of this and the body begins to waste, the hunter's razor senses are blunted. The advantage shifts increasingly to the side of the turkey, who greets each dawn perfectly refreshed and full of enthusiasm for his morning's duties.

The single mercy is that the season lasts only three weeks. By the end of it, the hunter, stumbling out of the nettles, mud-caked to the knees, eyes staring classily from a face smeared with a fortnight's layers of camouflage grease, is alarming to see. The flame of hope has burned low. His legs do not carry him straight forward any more. The thought of a whole night between sheets fills him with ungovernable emotion. He has forgotten why he went to the woods.

That's the condition in which I returned home, reeling from car to house and fumbling with my key at the lock.

"Where is he?" my wife said.

"Where's who?" I let fall my burden of guns, duffel, laundry, crusted boots and the other detritus of my happy days away, but managed to remain on my feet.

That heap of things did not include a turkey.

"I thought you told me his brain was –"

"That's right," I mumbled. "The size of an aspirin."

Tired as I was, I could not help noticing that she was looking at me in a clinical way. And that what appeared to interest her was the distance between my ears.

Summer

In a corner of the woods, a quiet retreat.
- Charles Porter photo

Dorothy and Hugh in the first happy years.

Charles, 1959, with his pitiful woodpile.

Two woodland orphans, Shorty and Slatz.

Anne and Jennie at the cabin, circa. 1974.
– James Scott photo

Equipped for comfort with rocker and stove.

A gallery of dear friends, rich memories.

Anne, in 2000, her first turkey.

17

Rain had washed the day. Then night came down, with the hint of a new storm flickering low in the southwest. In the last hour of light I'd gone out in the rowboat while she read in a chair on the pond dam. I'd promised fish for supper, and as it nearly always does, that friendly water had given them up willingly.

Now the filets browned and crisped in the iron skillet. We would eat, and after that ... afterward we would do exactly as we pleased. There were no obligations, no appointments to keep.

"Should I build a fire?"

"Maybe a little one," she said. "Just to take the chill off."

There we were at the start of summer, and glad for the comfort of the old wood stove that creaked with its warming.

"It feels like the mountains. A mountain cabin."

"Almost," I said.

"Like someplace a long way away."

The fish, hardly more than a half-hour from the pond, were wonderful. We wolfed them all.

"You know, I really believe we could start a restaurant with these."

"You'd have to catch *a lot* of fish," she said.

"Right. That's the good part."

We'd driven down that same afternoon, and we had only the one night and part of the next day to stay there. Before bed, I stepped outside to check the weather. The front had passed. The one to the south had not yet arrived, though its pulses of lightning were nearer. Flung across the dark directly above, between the leafy branches, was a glittering infinity of stars.

The truth is we were just two hours from our city home. But distance, like time, is mostly in the mind. For however long we were here, there would be no claims on us. And I thought of that later, as I lay listening to the wind begin to rise, waiting for sleep to come.

What charms us about these short excursions, and what makes them so refreshing, is the sense of separation – of having put just a bit of distance between ourselves and the too-well-known, the too-often-seen. But where is there, really, for anyone to go? Huddled all together on our dust mote of a planet, lost on a scale of distance too great to calculate or even imagine, we are, not just by habit but by our destiny, communal creatures.

We build our houses side by side, and are made uneasy by too far, too empty, a horizon. We touch hands in greeting. We gather eagerly in rooms full of noisy chatter, even when there's nothing new to say. Solitary confinement is, except for death, the most dreaded punishment. Too much isolation can drive us mad. It's only a sample of separation we want, to be reminded of its meaning without its consequences – the giddy view from the edge of the abyss, without the actual leap. And that doesn't require much of an expedition. Any humble place wrapped round by the stillness of uninterrupted time will suffice.

That night, in darkness, the wind whipped the branches at the roof's eave, the storm put out the far stars, the downpour came. And in the morning, after just long enough apart, we hurried back to the safety of the crowd.

18

Other beauty winners may come to sad ends on Hugh Hefner's couch or as centerfolds in lascivious magazines. But as far as anyone seems to know, the winners of the Appleton City Stout Baby Show all have turned out well.

The show has been held since 1903, on the day of the Appleton City, Missouri, annual fair. And a word of clarification is needed about its name, which has nothing to do with the heft of the entrants – although most babies do tend, by and large, toward stoutness. Stout was the name of the first winner, a boy. His parents collected a $2 cash prize and the congratulations of their fellow townsfolk. And in proud memory of that day, the Stout family has sponsored the show all these subsequent years, with only a brief interruption for the waging of a World War. I forgot to ask which war that was.

One evening not long ago our telephone rang and a pleasant voice on the other end inquired if my wife was the former Katie Jane Ingels, with Appleton City, Missouri, connections. She certainly was I replied. Her father grew up on a farm outside that pretty town. Her mother took a job there as a young school teacher. They met, married and moved to Jefferson City, but often came back to visit friends. A daughter was born to them – a bride to me.

"She was a Stout baby, wasn't she?" the caller asked.

"I didn't know her then," I told him. "But she's a nice, trim size now."

"No, no!" said the voice on the phone, "I mean a *Stout Baby Show* winner! The anniversary of the show is coming up. And we're having a reception for all the prize babies. We hope she can come."

"Haw!" I said.

"Beg pardon?"

"Nothing," I said. "The winning baby's right here, if you'd like to speak to her."

My wife noted the day, time and place. The reception, naturally, would be in the home of the successor Stouts. And she was to wear her medal if she could find it – which, as it turned out, she couldn't. It was a pin with a gold pendant that said "Prize Baby." Each year's winner got one, until the price of gold forced a switch to a silver cup.

After she hung up the phone, I made some wisecrack about this moment of past fame. She didn't laugh.

"What was the last beauty show you won?" was all she said.

Well, to shorten the tale, we did go. Appleton City is not far from our cabin and farm, and it was a pretty drive through that lush little pocket of country. Clouds raced overhead, and thriving fields

and dark woods spread away on every side. Then
the silver water tower of the town came in sight,
we found the street, the house, and went inside and
were greeted by Mrs. Stout, widow of the first
winner.

Mr. Stout's cradle, wicker high chair and some
of his starched smocks were displayed. There were
nice refreshments. And there was an album, with
photographs of the winners arranged by years. I
found the picture of my wife, at age 8 months – a
large-eyed infant, perched atop a cranberry crate
in a child's red wagon. And she was even then, I
freely admit, quite appealing.

Seventeen prize babies of all ages had come to
the reunion, many driving back from other places.
Looking around that room, you'd have to say they
all had lived up to their promise. The man who won
the year after my wife had come all the way from
Florida, with his young wife and their baby, a current entrant.

From the reception, then, we all adjourned to the
park for the unfolding of this year's drama. Quite
a crowd was there – a couple of hundred folks,

arranged on open-air bleachers in front of a raised stage. It was the last evening of the fair. Carnival roustabouts were readying the rides, and you could smell hamburgers that volunteers were grilling over a fire beside the concession stand.

The afternoon cooled. The year's baby crop – 41 contestants, all coiffed and ribboned and frilly – were displayed on the stage by beaming parents. The judges made notes. A winner was announced (although ranking babies is like choosing between perfect blossoms), and the Stout cup was presented. The crowd lingered, visiting, while a band began setting up its drums and amplifiers on the stage.

I thought of my wife, an infant those many summers ago. A great prize, still. And of her parents, young as they would have been then. The archaic sweetness of that day suddenly was powerfully affecting. One could do worse than to come from a place where people still gather together in public celebrations of lives beginning, the proof of a future assured.

19

The advantage of being rooted to a piece of land,
instead of being always a wanderer in the world,
is that you come to know all the most important
things about it: where the deer bed and the turkeys
nest their young, where the mushrooms appear, and
where the most prolific berry thickets grow. Over
the years you collect other bits of information, too.
But those are the most essential.

People long familiar with this piece of country
cannot remember a year when the blackberries began coming ripe so soon, or the canes were heavier
with fruit. No late frost caught them in the bloom.
And the summer's moisture has been, to say the
least, sufficient.

July the Fourth is the traditional day for the start
of picking. This year, by middle June, a full two
weeks early, the first were ready to be gathered.
Most still were red, so you had to search for the
ripe ones. But they were there, low amid the foliage - plump and glossy black, though a bit tart yet.
A few days more and they'll be sweeter, and by a

bit deeper into July nearly all will mature. The trick then will be to make the hand deliver them to the pail, not to the mouth.

I know of no gift that nature gives in greater abundance. Even in a poor year, usually there's some sheltered place whose microclimate has preserved enough for a pie or a cobbler or two. The gift is not free, of course. You pay for them in blood. In the same way you can tell a boxer by his crooked nose or a wrestler by his ears, berry pickers can be recognized by the sorry condition of their hands and arms.

But part of the attraction, I think, is that like so many of the best things they cost a certain amount of trouble and pain in the getting. The fattest berries always seem to be in places deep among the wickedest, thorniest tangles. I can remember more than once getting so snagged and entangled in the canes that there seemed no hope of ever getting loose again. And I was tempted to cry out to my fellow pickers just to go on and leave me, the way some northern tribes abandon their infirm alone on the ice, to await the mercy of predators.

Unfortunately, in that country there are few predators of sufficient size or savagery to finish the job. So there was nothing for it but to make my way to freedom in the best possible way, whimpering and using what I believe is termed adult language. And trying not to drop the part-full pail of berries already picked.

In truth, no piece of the anatomy is spared, since ticks and chiggers also love blackberries, and wait for you there in the bushes in inestimable numbers. Even in the city, when I was small, my mother dusted sulfur in my socks and inside my trousers to keep those pests away. It was useless. Then as now, no preparation I know of would turn them – the chiggers especially. It's said one also ought to be careful of snakes in a blackberry thicket, though I've never met one there.

But the suffering goes with it. If you want your berries cheap, buy tame ones at the store. They're edible – the way eggs from commercial chickens are edible, though they can't compare with the brown-speckled ones laid by free-range country hens.

On a recent morning, with my wife and daughters, I set off through the woods toward the back pasture, where the biggest and most dependable thickets are. The day was pleasant, with a fine breeze and a thin drift of clouds holding back the early sun. In the valley below the old farmhouse we followed the stream past the pebble-bottomed pool where, when they were toddlers, our daughters stopped to splash on a summer day.

I could hear again, as if it were yesterday, their cries of delight at the coldness of the clear water.

Up a stony hill from the valley, we passed into the back hay field. At least that's what it has been for many years. When I saw it first it was a long-fallow piece of useless ground, grown up in sprouts and weeds. I remembered what labor it took to tame that feral meadow. And the antique tractor and other derelict equipment we had to use. And the man who worked beside me – a man of the hills, whose life and luck had been very different from my own, but who came to be as close as the brother I never had. It's been more than three decades since he went to lie with his brothers in a country churchyard not far away.

What I felt, in recalling those times, was not so much regret as just astonishment at how near they seemed, in spite of all the years that have elapsed.

We crossed the field, then, and in the line of thickets strung out along its edge above the pond the berries were as plentiful as I'd imagined. We each had a pail for gathering, but had filled them only a third of the way before the sun burned through the clouds. The breeze fell, the day turned sweltering and we had to stop.

It used to be I couldn't quit until my bucket was full to its top, and would stay until I was dizzy from the heat, with salt stinging my eyes and hands a bleeding ruin. But if the years have taught me anything at all, it's that you don't have to pick the patch clean. We'd gotten more than enough already for the pies we planned to bake, and the berries you gather toward the season's end are the sweetest ones by far.

We had some of them the next day, with dear country friends, beside an open window in the rain. And they were wonderful – as fine as anything you ever tasted. Where you find them, whom you pick them with and, afterward, whom you share them with, has a lot to do with the flavor of wild blackberries.

20

There's no explaining such a day of autumn light in summer. A gift without reason, that's what it was.

Cool the morning began, the air blue, the pale sky cloudless. Presently the sun climbed above the trees and began its march toward afternoon. But, oddly, this day, it was not a thing afire. Where it fell directly, there was only a pleasant warmth. And in every shadow was a sudden coolness. That's how the light is in the high mountains. Or in the forest of the far north. Or in the shank of a fine October in the midlands, with the year in quick decline.

But this was the dead of summer – a month in the midlands whose days are rarely sweet. My daughters, the old dog and I were prepared to suffer some, but received, instead, the gift of that miracle day.

We did all the old things. Fished the pond, which sparkled with the rush of sudden little winds across it. Took aimless walks. Built fires for cooking over. Heard the red-winged blackbirds whistling from the reeds. Listened to the unaccustomed stillness of our hearts.

The old dog, who at home can barely climb the stair, scampered like a pup. She swam twice across the pond, then, grinning, swam a creek. And you could tell she was remembering how it was before the soreness came.

We remembered, too. Recalled the people – gone – whose shadows walk those woods. And remembered the day we began, together, the building of the tree house. We still think of the tree house as new, but the girls were small then, and now they're grown. So something in our chronology is flawed.

It will not be many years before they'll both be away to somewhere – some other city, or some other place in the world – to discover the further shape of their lives. The old dog has cataracts, and has gotten deaf. One day the stair will defeat her.

My own legs tire sooner than they used to. The changes start to be a load to carry.

How many more such country days? we thought, though no one asked it aloud. Sometimes we just stopped, still as stones, to wonder at the peculiar quality of the light shining on the plump hay bales, on the curious cow faces across a fence. The trees at field's edge were drawn as in a painting, their shadows black. Then evening came, and veils of ground fog rose and flowed across the land. And in the darkness we drove nearly 50 miles to find ice cream to put the berries over, thus achieving the final perfection.

You're lucky if, in a whole lifetime, there are just a few days that fill you up that way. Nearly everything we did, we'd done before. But it was different this time. This time, beside the pleasure, there was about each moment a sense of conclusion – no, of *completion*.

The feeling had something to do with that strange summer day of autumn light, reflecting off leaf and water, reflecting off the memories of gathered years, in this season of all our uncertain passages.

21

Twenty steps or so east of the junction of two county roads is the gate to my cabin drive. The cinnamon-brown dog was curled at the gatepost, as if waiting for his people to come home. We weren't his people. But we knew a friendly dog when we met one, so on the next trip to town we laid in a modest supply of kibbles. Just enough to see him through until the real owners showed up.

Sure enough, the phone rang. It was a neighbor calling from a short way up the road. "There's a man here that says he's lost his dog. Says it's a brown dog. Have you seen one?"

"As a matter of fact, I'm looking at it right now. He just showed up yesterday."

"Good," the neighbor said. "I'll send the fellow over."

The man parked out on the road and walked up the drive to the clearing.

"That's not my dog."

"He's brown. And he's a good dog."

"That don't matter! He's not mine! Mine was a kinda sheepdog." The man sounded half mad about it. And turning on his heel, he left.

The brown dog stayed. We had to call him something, so we named him Lucky. It seemed to fit. Anything that shows up at that road corner is in luck. Twenty years or more ago, I thought I saw a white piece of paper in the grass of the lane that runs down to the pond. But when I went to pick it up, the paper turned out to be a small white kitten, dirty, lost and hungry. I named her Lucky, too, fed her milk, brought her to the city. A friend took her, and over the years she was much prized.

This new Lucky won't have any offspring. Whoever had him and lost him at least cared enough to have him neutered. But it was clear he'd been awhile on his own. He was covered with mites, his ribs showed, and when a bowl of food was set before him he inhaled it quicker than you can read this.

We couldn't just leave him. The fox vixen and her kits might still be spending time under the cabin. Dogs and foxes don't mix any better than dogs and roads. So, like the first Lucky, he came back to town with us, and stopped off with Dan, our longtime veterinarian friend, to be examined and doctored as needed.

The reports were all good. He tested free of any diseases. Several dippings rid him of the mites. Regular feeding made the sharp ribs disappear. He'd had no schooling, and jumped up with a youngster's joy on anyone he thought might be a pal. That small defect was offset by a handsome smooth coat, warm brown eyes and a fine toothy smile. But Lucky needed one further piece of luck – a real home.

So I started to write a column about him for the paper, saying he came with no liens, unpaid bills or other baggage. Just enthusiasm and a good appetite. Before I could finish that piece I was at a literary affair in a library. Good things invariably happen in libraries.

I met there a wonderful couple – Joe and Judy are their names – who live on an acreage well outside the city. We got to talking about our pets, and Judy mentioned they'd recently lost a dear dog to age, and were down to two.

"That's not enough," she said. "We need another dog."

I thought an angel had spoken, and I told her about Lucky.

"He's not perfect," I said, wanting to be honest.

"Who needs perfect?"

"He jumps up on folks."

"That's nothing!" she replied.

You can guess the rest.

22

All night the rain beat down, the thunder rolled. And morning broke gloomy-dark. But we'd been trying for two weeks to get away for a little fishing, one daughter and I. So just on speculation, ignoring the weather, we traveled the two hours south to the cabin – the first part through pelting showers.

As we left the main highway to travel country roads the sky lightened, clouds began to roll away to the east, and scraps of blue could be seen through the gray. By the time we turned in the drive, the murk had cleared away entirely. We unloaded gear, then went to pay a visit to a friend three miles along the road. Finally, at midday, we got to the business at hand.

Sometime earlier that week a wind had blown down a tree across the lane to the cabin pond. So first I had to fetch the chain saw and clear the way. Then, with rods, tackle box and oars in the back of the car, we drove down to that little gem of a fishing hole my two daughters have known for all their lives, and I for much of mine.

The pond - a half-acre at most in size - is surrounded on all sides by woods. At the water's edge are thickets of wild rose, rich with pink bloom in season, and tangles of blackberry canes. Along the east bank, and spotted through the forest to the north, are some of those pine trees my wife and I planted with friends the month before we were married. That was in 1966. The pines are grown as tall as 50 feet now, some of them more.

Even earlier than that, in 1960, the pond was stocked. And from that time until now it has been amazingly productive both of pleasure and of dinners. I fished it with my parents, and with friends in all the years since. It was there that my daughters, when they were 6 and 7, began to learn the use of spinning and fly rods. They're good company in a boat, and as capable as any man I know.

Many years ago - dust-covered and exhausted after a long, blistering day of harvesting wheat - I went down in the evening to cool off and make a few casts at the pond. Just at dark I caught and held briefly in my hand the largest bass I have ever seen alive or dead.

I released that wonderful fish, hoping one of my girls would sometime catch her. But, of course, we never saw her again.

Above all, though, that small piece of water has been remarkable for its production of hand-size bluegills, those spirited and brightly colored panfish that are as fine for sport as they are for the table. Those were what my daughter and I were after that recent day, and were what we found. One after another, sometimes on successive casts, they rose to the small yellow artificial flies we offered.

Too quickly the afternoon went by, as perfect times are apt to do.

But days like that never really are lost. They are forever stored away in memory – the freshness of the weather, the clarity of light, the joy of companionship – to be called back if a time comes when they are needed, as sooner or later they are sure to be.

23

Beyond the pavement and the sirens, out here where lives are governed by the angle of the sun, one senses more clearly the first delicate signs of the season beginning to change.

Whoever the lodger was who'd scratched and bumped at night under the floor in recent weeks has left to prepare an autumn den in the forest, and grass has grown in the entry between the foundation stones.

Clouds of minnows, summer's last hatch of them, move like shifting smoke in the shallows of the pond.

A neighbor told of watching a red fox transfer her three kits from their den under his pig shed to new quarters next to his hay barn. He went up to investigate. One of the youngsters, the boldest, came out, inspected the man-creature at a distance of five steps, then scratched a flea, yawned, and lay down to sun, paying him no further notice.

On such days as these, it's hard to imagine anything going very wrong.

We spent part of a recent afternoon walking through a wooded valley I haven't visited in springtime for several years. There'd been a morning shower. Then the clouds had rushed away to the south, and the day turned fine. The trees in that valley are straight and tall, their canopy closing overhead so the woodland floor is largely free of undergrowth. Light filtering down through the new leaves made the air itself seem luminous green. A small brook runs down from the upper meadows and meanders through the forest there. Several seep springs feed it, so that even during the stifle of summer it manages to flow a trickle. In this season, though, it is bright and lively as a mountain stream, rushing around fallen logs and over stones with a sound like happy conversation. We came to a place where the brook widened and deepened to make a little pool.

"You won't remember," I told my daughter, "but a long time ago, when you and your sister were very small, we brought you here to wade. On a day a lot like this." It surprised me that she did remember across so many years She remembered the coldness of the water, and the smoothness of the stones under her feet.

"There's something else I want to show you," I said. And I led the way a bit farther along the valley, to where the tree stood rooted in the rich, dark soil between two branchings of the stream.

"It's a black walnut," I told her. "An exceptional one."

Her eyes traveled up its trunk, straight as a plumb line, 30 feet or more to the first branch. When first I found that tree I could reach around it easily. Now my hands fell several inches short of meeting.

"It's funny," I told her. "I've thought for a long time about putting a dam across the lower end of this valley. It would have made a wonderful lake. But I never could do it."

"Because of one tree?"

"Partly that. It's a wonderful tree – worth some money. A log like that would go to Japan, and be cut into sheets of veneer for making furniture."

"Why don't you sell it, then, and build your lake?"

The whole reason was more complicated, having also to do with the rest of the valley, and memories fixed there, like the one of two little girls in the pool, and of friends I'd walked with in the coolness of that place. The great walnut just made explaining simpler.

"Because," I said, "if nothing happens to it – a fire, a lightning strike – someday that tree will be worth a great deal of money. In your lifetime, and your sister's."

Ordinarily we steer around the subject of time's passage, too much talk of which can put a shadow over the moment. But on a day as fine as that one, in the season of everything starting to feel new again, there was no sense of danger in the longer considerations.

24

If it were possible to special-order another two perfect days at the end of summer, those are the two I'd choose.

The sun of the first afternoon was bright but gentle, the woodland shadows as crisp and dark as in some countryside much farther north. At evening, the cabin pond was a mirror, disturbed only by the splash of oars and the circles made by fish rising. The pale sky yielded an early star, then a speckling of them. From the circling forest came the sleepy nocturnes of birds just going to roost. Bullfrogs cleared their throats among the reeds.

One of our daughters is leaving soon, outbound for a year of study in a foreign place. She and I had taken the chance to slip away overnight to that humble little place in the corner of the woods that holds, for all of us, so many memories. It's less than a week, now, before she goes – no time at all. A year is long. The passage from abstract planning to the urgency of going has been astonishingly quick.

Mostly, in our time together, we talked. Some of the talk was about the future, and her adventure that lies ahead. More was about things past, people remembered.

In the uneven relationships of parents and their young, so much energy is spent on redefining changed roles and dealing with the awkward and sometimes painful process of letting go that little chance is left for uncluttered retrospect. The moments for it have to be manufactured.

That's what we'd done, out of some need we'd felt in common. And we spent our scrap of time frugally, as you do when you're reminded how fast the clock of our lives is turning.

We fished a bit, and caught almost nothing – but were absolutely sure that the point of it was to be in the boat at that hour, watching the night come down, drawing on the saved capital of so many other nights on that and other waters. We cooked over an outdoor fire after dark. I burned the meat and we pronounced it done to perfection.

A little breeze came up and freshened the air for sleeping.

Awake again at half-past 5 o'clock, we watched the first light come. And, walking down to the water, startled a wild duck nesting at the edge. The sky blackened, and a noisy rainstorm came marching across the timbered hills. We watched that through the screen of the cabin porch. The mingled smell of rain and earth was powerful and strange.

A few short minutes more and the storm had rushed away eastward, letting the sun strike a washed sparkle on every blade and leaf.

We went for breakfast, and visited some country friends, and napped away the tiredness of that early rising. And talked some more. Then set the cabin straight – not so much a labor as a rite of devotion. And then, across the fat and gem-green countryside, drove home.

And that was all.

We did nothing, really. We did exactly everything we cared to. With a completeness that will make

the later words perfunctory, a year's goodbyes have
been said to the satisfaction of us both.

25

Provoked by something I cannot explain, unless
perhaps it is the change in the pattern of our lives
with our daughters gone, I have come to a decision
that's been long deferred.

For thirty years now – not quite half my life – I
have imagined a lake in that valley on the farm. The
place is where two steep draws join to make a quar-
ter-mile-long basin that pinches down at the end to
a narrow neck, an ideal dam site, The drainage into
the larger draw is from the south, out of a field of
native grass. The other receives the runoff from hay
ground to the west. None of that land is tilled, or
ever will be – not in my ownership, at least.

Besides rainfall, the streams are fed by springs.
Many of those are only trickles. But one, dependable even in the driest times, is walled up with
rocks. It is said that settlers passing through used

to camp there, and water themselves and their stock on the way to more promising country. In a grove of cedars on open, higher ground are 15 or 20 unmarked field stones set on edge to mark the burying places of some who could not go on.

The valley itself, from the lower slopes all the way up to the beginning of the fields, is prettily wooded, mostly with white and red oaks. Some of those are splendid and very old. There also are many cedars, several large sycamores and shag-bark hickories, but the oaks dominate.

Once, during the long drive back from a vacation in Mexico, during times when my wife was at the wheel, I even sketched out on a tablet how I thought the lake would look, and where someday a cottage might be situated on the shore.

I never got beyond the dreaming, though. Two things stopped me, and one was money. It used to be thought that newspaper folk were best kept clinging white-knuckled to the brink of poverty, lest they get too fancy a notion of themselves. It's hard to squirrel away enough to build a lake by padding receipts from cab rides and greasy-spoon lunches.

But more than finances, what put the idea on hold - and you may think this silly - was one single tree, that wonderful walnut standing in the crotch of the valley's Y, on a little plot of loamy ground washed down to where the two streams join. Towering over all else, it is a spectacular example of the species. Around it are others it has seeded out, some of them decent trees in their own right. But that one is the patriarch. It has given me pleasure every time I've walked that way, crossing on my way to a high meadow on the other side.

Last fall a wildfire raged across my land, devouring fields and scarring the woodland in a way that sickened the heart. When it had passed and the ground had cooled, I hiked down into the valley, expecting the worst. In that hideous landscape of ashes and ruin, there was a single small island of unblackened ground, around which the fire unaccountably had passed.

In the very center, perfectly untouched, stood the grand walnut tree. Pure luck it was, clarifying for a layman what every forester knows. Trees' lives have limits, just as ours do, and are shadowed by hazards, of which fire is only one. Winds can topple and break them. Lightning can splinter them. In the end, all perish and fall.

I decided in that moment that the lake would be built after all.

It's a serious thing to fell such a tree. It will not be wasted. Almost certainly it will be made into furniture, to give pleasure for generations. In my mind I see the lake as it will be – almost 15 acres of water, flanked by wooded hillsides. I see the morning fog eddying, and autumn leaves afloat like ships. I hear the splash of big fish rising and the windy rush that ducks' wings make as they wheel into the wind for landing.

Life, as they say, is choices. But fine as all that will be, and much as I will love that piece of water, I think that I will always feel a bit of sadness about the tree.

26

I'd been tied up much of the afternoon with country business. Somehow time had gotten away, and I'd considered not fishing at all. But then I remembered what a man once said about hunting: that a day when you might have followed the dog, but didn't, was a day you'd never see again. So there I was, rod in hand, dropping the bass bug close against the reeds. There'd be time for two, maybe three circuits of the shoreline.

This one was a different pond – the one we call the bean field pond, situated in the corner of an acreage we used to farm. Built some 40 years ago, it is deep and clear, fed by runoff from what is now untilled grassland, it has been wonderfully productive. I have fished it not only with my daughters, through all their ages, but also with a good many friends.

Even when I'm by myself those memories are with me in the boat.

A cool front had dipped down from the northern

plains, bringing with it a badly needed rain. Even as I'd pushed the johnboat out from the bank and through the cattails there had come a last pelting of big drops. Then that shower blew on past as well, and the sky began showing broken patches of blue. Except for birdsong and the creaking of the oarlocks, the silence was absolute. A handsome little snake, green as emerald, etched his sinuous way across the surface just ahead.

It's curious, how little a fisherman's excitement changes through the years. The skipped heartbeat when the fish's weight is first felt and line is stripped from the reel in that initial bullish run. The thrill's no different today than it was in boyhood. What's changed is that the catching matters less, especially since nearly all those brought to boat are freed to grow and give battle another day. It's enough to be attached for a while – to feel that wildness at the leader's end.

This one was a female largemouth, heavy-bodied, a wonder of a fish. I grasped her lower lip and slipped the hook free without lifting her from the water. Released, she sank away and vanished with a flash. One like that is enough. I put down the

rod and took up my coffee, gone cold in the cup.
The late sun had dropped below what remained
of clouds, and threw long shadows of the cattails
dark across the glassy pond. The color of the water
changed with the sky, deepening finally to purple.
A bullfrog boomed from the near shore. From
across the way a rival answered.

That's a fine hour, just before the light goes out,
but also a melancholy one. You think of everything
and everyone, happy things and sad – of times
gone, and people gone, and mistakes made, and
chances of one kind or other let slip away. And it's
always then, with darkness closing, that one would
be most grateful for a little company. But there
wasn't any. So, not lingering longer, I rowed ashore,
pulled the boat up and hurried to the car.

One ought to fish in the early mornings, when
the first light is just coming and the whole day lies
bright ahead, I was thinking then.

Or else not fish alone.

Autumn

27

I love the autumn – as I love some of the people in my life – for the sharpness of her moods.

An even nature is often praised as a high virtue. The people who say that wear sensible shoes, reconcile their checkbooks monthly, and wouldn't speak up at their own executions for fear of saying something that might give offense. But autumn, bless her, makes a fuss. (In the mind, if not in the language of the French, autumn and spring are of the feminine gender, summer sexless, and winter – like snakes – always masculine. I can't say why, but it's literary fact.)

On a recent evening, one of those sudden moods was coming on. The forecast was for drizzle and cold, but standing outside in the last hour of light you hardly could believe it. From just below the horizon, the sun sent up a blaze of apricot behind the thinning latticework of trees. Overhead, a bank of clouds driven by some mighty wind aloft slid away to eastward like a curtain drawn, opening the view into an eternity of deepest blue.

The night was sweet and warm, with no sign yet of the change. It was coming, though. Extravagance like that seldom is accidental or wasted. And while we slept, the chill blew in. That's autumn for you – willful, abrupt, preferring intensity and surprise to ingratiation.

Somehow, this sudden change swept clutter away, clarified memory. All through that first cold day I was awash in things and people powerfully recalled. A house we used to live in. The sense of us still young. Those two little hounds I loved. My father alive. Friends as they were before time or circumstance got in the way. The excitement of writing before it got so hard.

Also the bite of cold mornings through a canvas coat, with mallards working to the call or quail exploding from the frosty grass. The treehouse when it was new. Our children small, and bedtime readings beside the slatted cribs. The song of their laughter, when they'd not yet learned the possibilities of grief.

That's part of what I'm able to retrieve in this season of the year. It must be something in the mix of weather and the changing light, because it happens every fall. No other passage excites me so. I know that some people approach autumn full of dread and melancholy. I come to her, each time, breathless as a boy hurrying to meet his life's first love again.

28

An intruder, approaching from the back way through the woods, will have heard nothing like it before. The electronic chirping will sound faintly at first, its source a mystery. But as the scoundrel draws nearer, coming into the clearing, the chirp will become a piercing warble.

And as he rounds the corner of the cabin, the warble will amplify into a pulsing howl – filling his head, addling his senses and sending him back to whatever dark hole he came from. At least that is how it is supposed to work. We'll soon know if there's anything to the claim.

This season, with the weather hardening, is when

a country place invites trespass. I don't speak here of the neighbors, who are decent folk, not generally given to breaking and entering. The problem is deer mice. They come out of the forest in irresistible waves, and almost nothing will turn them.

You may despise their intrusion, but you have to admire their resourcefulness. They gnaw through walls. Once indoors, they find their way inside cabinets and dressers and onto high shelves. The coming winter will be long, and their appetite is prodigious for beasts so small. They will devour any foodstuffs not encased in glass or metal. One year I left a package of dry spaghetti on a shelf above the stove. When I opened the cabin the next spring, there was a stash of spaghetti in the pocket of every coat and shirt in the closet.

They will shred towels, clothing and magazines, or eviscerate feather pillows, to make nests of fluff for their young. And whatever may be said for or against them, they are enthusiastic breeders. I read somewhere that the deer mouse achieves sexual maturity in a matter of only months, and that a female is capable of producing twelve litters a year of four to six infants each – for a possible total of 40-some

to more than 60 or 70. That certainly squares with
the experience I've had with mice. They are nothing
if not libidinous.

Put out traps, and when you come back a week
or a month later the traps have all been sprung,
but the mice are more numerous than before. As I
have mentioned before, the man whose crude shack
became the nucleus of my enlarged cabin used to
lie drunk on his cot and shoot at them with a pistol.
With the remodeling we've done, that's behavior I
discourage.

Anyway, taken in the singular – though because
of their lechery they rarely are singular for more
than a few minutes at a time – deer mice are quite
handsome little creatures. As a control measure,
gunfire seems excessive. Instead, mounted on the
inside wall just above the door is a fabulous inven-
tion, smaller than a toaster.

It's an ultrasound anti-mouse machine, which according to the literature also is effective against spi-
ders, bugs and bats. This amazing device came as a
gift from a friend, who used to live in Alaska. It has
three settings. The first is at a frequency inaudible

to humans or other higher mammals but reportedly unpleasant for mice. The second can be heard and is mildly annoying. The third setting is for when the place is not in use. Prolonged exposure to that one will stimulate the growth of facial hair, shake fillings out of teeth and produce ungovernable lunacy.

The Alaskan winters were long, my friend said, and every year, when the world went dark, he was overrun by a plague of mice. Then he put up one of these, plugged it in and switched it on high. And after that he never had another mouse. Or another houseguest.

We'll see how the thing works at my cabin in the woods.

29

Our day afield together was framed by flights of geese.

The first hint of morning light found us on a stone ledge, looking down into a wooded hollow through

which I have walked a hundred times. A short way
to our right were the tumbled foundation stones of a
settler house. Beyond, pale between the trees at the
valley's edge, was a meadow of rank grass running
down to another wood line. It's a corner of the farm
she had not seen before – a magical place, where
the narrative of centuries is compressed.

Hunting parties of Osage Indians certainly
camped in the rock shelter under the bluff at the
valley's side. Then some rugged interloper came to
dull his plow and break himself on the stony ground
above.

Later, farmers enlarged the fields, and, after
them, I arrived to fence the place. Now time has
defeated me, as it did the others. Nothing has lasted
except the smoke-blackening in the cave shelter
from the first hunters' fires. Apart from that, none of
us has left any durable mark.

"It's beautiful here," she said, her view unclouded by all those earlier failures and the rush of years.

And, as she spoke, the first far-off cries came
down to us from the skeins of snow and blue geese,

outbound against the high morning breeze toward their day's first feed. Faces turned skyward, we watched the sparkle of them in the new sun, the ragged lines shifting like threads of blown smoke against the cloudless blue.

Do they ever imagine falling? I wondered to myself. Does it occur to them that they could someday lose their way?

Our outing was very near perfection. She'd been away at college in a distant place – a voice drawn thin by the telephone wire. So this was the first year in five we'd been able to watch the autumn turn together. And after some miserable days, this one had arrived mild and fine. We were there when the squirrels came out sleepily on their branches. We were startled by the racket the turkeys made when they came thundering off their roosts. We sat until we tired of sitting, then walked a couple of miles and took our time to do it. And at midday – incredible luxury – we napped.

Skip forward several hours, now.

It is the end of afternoon, and we are at a different place on the land, where a field declines to a wooded corner and a pond. The hard breeze has laid, and a sweet, profound stillness has replaced the rustle of grass and leaves. We are watching for deer, which do not come. The deer are only an excuse for being there.

And again the geese are heard, inbound toward their night's resting place. This time they are riding down the long hill of sky on slow wings, not beating into a headwind. In wave after wave they keep coming – so many that they take most of half an hour to pass. I am thinking that, just as anything alive, they too are governed by time and losses. And yet, midway on their dangerous passage, the survivors fill the air with their cries of collective joy. And by the very number of their voices, they declare the future secure.

I look across to my daughter, where she sits against a tree.

"My heart's full," I tell her. It requires no explanation.

Face and hair brushed by the last orange light, she answers with a nod.

30

Inspectors from a consumer watchdog group dropped in recently to see how government guidelines were being followed at a certain country cafe, the Tub O' Lard, where folks of my rural neighborhood regularly assemble.

It was the breakfast hour, and the place was wall-to-wall with farmers in coveralls and hunters in orange jackets, all calling out for their morning ration of grease. You could spot the inspectors right away by their suits and ties and the clipboards they were carrying. The waitress, Bobbie Sue, put their plates in front of them.

"Excuse me, young lady," one of them said to her. "Could you tell me at what temperature these eggs were cooked?"

"Over easy," she told him. "Like you asked."

"No," he said. "I mean the actual cooking temperature."

Mornings at the Tub O' Lard get pretty busy, and Bobbie Sue didn't have a lot of time for foolishness.

"Hey, Thelma," she bawled back in the general direction of the kitchen, where the cook was setting new orders up in the window. "Fella out here's got a question."

Every head in the place turned to look at the table of suits.

"Wants to know how hot is his eggs."

A titter passed through the crowd.

"Never mind," the man said. "I'll see for myself."

He took a small black case from his pocket, got out a thermometer and thrust the end of it into the liquid yolk of one of his eggs-over-easy. Then he wrote something down on his clipboard.

"That just won't do," he said, tapping the paper with his finger. "And I see where the lunch special is fried chicken. I'm also very concerned about that."

"What's he sayin' now?" the cook, Thelma, called from the kitchen.

"He's worried about your chicken."

The cook replied with a word that can't be printed here, and the men in coveralls and orange jackets all laughed out loud.

"You tell him I been fryin' chicken longer'n he's been alive," she cried out indignantly. "And there hasn't been no complaints yet."

"That's right," several of the regulars said.

"You bet! Best damned chicken any place around!"

The mood in the place was beginning to tense up.

"One more thing," the inspector told Bobbie Sue. "When were you last tested for communicable diseases?"

"Say what?"

"If you wouldn't mind, I'd like to see your current health certificate."

"Lordy!" said the waitress, and she threw up her hands in hopelessness. "Now he's saying maybe I got something nasty."

That was the last straw. Bobbie Sue was a great favorite there at the Tub O' Lard. A general grumble was heard, and some of the other patrons, several of them rather large, started to get up from their chairs.

"Never mind," said the inspector. "Just let us have our check."

31

Usually, when I go to the country, what I find are problems to be dealt with, some crisis to be deflected. Another fence is down. Or some neighbor has a grievance with me, or I with him. That's how it's been, and how it will be again. It's the nature, dependable as drought and taxes, of men's endeavors on the land.

But for this day all such concerns were suspended.

The year's hay was made, the bales arranged in rows at the woods' edge. Fields mowed at the start of summer had regrown dark and lush, waiting to have cattle in them. Hawks wheeled in a cloudless sky. Quail called from the fence rows. Trees threw long, cool shadows. Blackbirds passed over in flocks like blowing smoke.

The only casualty was a single mouse, who'd gotten in a food package, then tried to slake his thirst in the commode, resulting in his life's last and longest swim.

With everything in such amazing order, we took a little time to try the pond. The fish are unpredictable as the season draws down. But this day we found them feeding – enough smaller ones to make our supper, then a big one that slid out from his hide beneath a bush to gulp the floating lure.

He made a long, strong run or two, jumped once heavily, then my daughter lifted him from the water.

"I think he's the biggest bass I ever caught," she said.

"He may be. He's a fine, great fish."

I carefully removed the hook, and he suspended for a moment in the water beside the boat, not understanding he was free. Then, in one powerful movement, vanished to grow another year.

Our final project was to prowl a bit in the woods, pulling down wild grapevines for material to make a wreath for the door at home. It should be an enormous one, we decided. After such a fish, anything small seemed hardly worth the trouble. When the berries of the bittersweet turn orange, we'll weave some of that in among the vines. And whatever seed pods we can find. We might tie on a dry ear of corn or two. And possibly a hornet's nest – less the hornets – if one of those should come to hand. Maybe even a Volkswagen or a Yugo.

The wreath we have planned will require several men to carry. That's the kind of extravagance such a day inspires.

I can't recall – and take pains to try not to – how many times I've driven the road back from there, frenzied and despairing at some catastrophe I've left behind. A machine stands broken in the field where I've abandoned it. Or brutal summer has left the autumn landscape parched to dust. An animal has strayed. Or someone I've depended on has let me down. Or, more often, I've been betrayed by some folly of my own.

Then, in a single day of quiet miracles, all the disappointments are canceled out. That's only illusion, of course. But one needs to save these rare exceptions, if one can, as insurance against the certainty of storms.

32

For those of us who invest our years and a piece of our hearts in woodland cabins, this darkening season holds three perils: mice, freeze and fire. The least of those is mice. They're a nuisance, but they're bearable. A greater hazard, as autumn comes on, is a sudden freeze.

Some cabins – mine is one – although technically "modern," have water systems of a frail kind, whose exposed pipes must be drained before hard weather sets in for good. One watches the forecast, and gambles a bit, trying to defer the draining until the last possible day. But sometimes a bitter front blows in unannounced. The temperature plummets overnight from the 70s into the teens, and the problems that result from a burst water pipe will make you forget completely the trifling damage a mouse can do.

Even so, flood is not the largest fear. The third danger is the worst.

The telephone message was left while we were out. *"We have a raging fire down here,"* the recording said. *"It's taken the shed and the doghouse. The cabin's scorched. One side is smoldering."*

A crew from the rural electric company had strung a new wire along the road frontage, and, when powering up the line, failed to notice another wire touching it. On the windiest day of the driest autumn in recent memory, the shorted wire fell sparking into the grass, and sent a wildfire out of control through my cabin clearing and on across the land.

 For as long as I've known that corner of the world – more than 50 years now – I have dreaded the fire season. And fires there've been, all around, but never until now on my cabin ground. Not knowing what, if anything, was left, we raced down the highway and along smaller roads. The great smudge of smoke on the horizon could be seen from nearly 20 miles away.

 The cabin still stood. Its sides were charred. But everything that mattered more – all the pictures and memories stored inside that little place – had miraculously been spared. The fire had burned through the wire that powered the well pump. But using the only vessel they could find, and getting water from the pressure tank on the porch, neighbors had splashed the outer walls and saved the structure.

 Baled hay had burned in the fields. Corner posts had been reduced to ash and fences were down. But such things can be replaced or mended. No houses or livestock had been lost, no people hurt. More than a day later, nearly two miles away – well beyond any land of mine – the fire still was burning. Volunteer departments had come from several communities around, and though they could not stop the fire, they'd managed to contain it. Soot-covered and red-eyed from smoke and chronic sleeplessness, those volunteers will be the real heroes of autumn all across that reach of country.

Thirsty as the woods and grasslands are, it could be weeks before the hazard passes.

33

We left the car at the farmhouse, climbed a metal gate and set off on foot to look over a new piece of land we'd been able to add. The grassy trail descended through a corner of woods to a little field. We could see from their prints that deer had been that way before us.

The leaves of the oaks spinning down through mellow sunlight made a sound like gentle rain. The air was just a little fresh. It was a fine day for a ramble.

"This first field's called what?" asked one of my daughters. "Is it the Flood Field?"

"That's right. Then, after the creek crossing, there's the long, narrow field we call the Neck."

Other people in their time no doubt had different names for them, but that doesn't matter – any more than it matters whether a street is called Elm or Locust. Names are only a shared code, so people can speak to one another about where they're going or where they've been. In wet years, when the floodgates are closed in the dam of Truman Lake, the reservoir that used to be a river, water backs up to cover the little field. And although that's happened only twice in memory, it's now the Flood Field, wet year or dry.

The Mountain Field has a peculiar stony knob at its upper end, and is less a mountain than what a South African would call a *kopje* – a limestone hillock rising sharply out of the surrounding land. Buzzards nest in a cleft on its east side, and the thicket of saplings at its base is a good place for finding vines of bittersweet. From the top, the view is unobstructed across the descending field to the

creek bottom and a far ridge. And there's a feeling
of being very high, although the true elevation is
not more than 30 feet above the adjoining terrain.

Beyond the Mountain Field, continuing on to
the east, is the Cave Meadow, called that because
there's a stone bluff in the valley just past it, with
the cave shelter that we imagine Indian hunting
parties must once have used.

Or, going the opposite direction from the mountain, there's the Deer Meadow – a slanting open
place of native grass and sumac where deer ought
to be seen, even if they usually aren't.

And so forth.

I like the way both girls are committing to mem
ory all the landmark names on the new property, so
that if the time comes when my legs won't carry me
there they can tell me where they've been. I'll know
exactly which location they speak of, and all the
pictures will come as clear to mind as in a photo-
graph.

We saw the place where a big buck had made his

scrapes at the woods' edge along the Neck. We tried to decide – depending on the direction of the wind – where it would be possible to conceal oneself in the first blue hour of morning to see him pass. Then we retraced our way back up to the farmhouse, where my friend was repairing a fence in the barn lot – work not so much for its own sake as to help him deal with an agony of worry.

His wife, companion of most of his years, was in the hospital in the town not far away. Nights and parts of every day he spent there with her. Chores like that bit of fencing helped pass the other hours. You could tell, from the deliberate, discouraged way he came walking down to meet us, that there wasn't news of much improvement to tell. We were sorry, and told him so. There's not much else anyone can do.

I asked if he was taking care of himself. Was he eating?

"Such as it is," he said.

"Tell her we're thinking of her."

"I will."

He went back to his fencing, then, and we left
to drive the highway home. It was clear, from the
silence in the car, how saddened my daughters
were. I think the young are alarmed at the problems
and griefs of people getting older because those are
losses that can't be governed or slowed.

Then, as you move toward that time yourself,
you begin to see the process not as something malicious and personal, but as part of the logic that rules
everything alive from grubs to men – a cause for
regret, maybe, but not for bitterness.

Why else would it matter to me that they learn
the names I've given to the fields and other features
of that piece of land, except for understanding that
we're so temporary on it?

34

"I've figured it out," said my wife.

"Figured what out? The riddle of the universe?"

"I've figured out why you go into the woods every November, and eat greasy food, use coarse language and drink from bottles."

"Because it's deer season," I said. "Isn't that obvious."

"No. It's because your middle name is Wesley."

"What the devil are you talking about?"

"It's perfectly clear," she said. "If you had a middle name like Hank, or Harley, or Bubba, I'm sure you would be content to cook, or raise African violets, or do something else civilized and useful."

"Don't be crazy!"

"Or crochet. I have read how professional football players, who weigh 300 pounds and are real men, sit around in their hotel rooms the night before the game and crochet doilies and tablecloths."

"It's a fiction," I said. "They have fingers like sausages."

"Or maybe it's needlepoint. But no, you got a middle name about which you feel insecure. So you have to go out in the woods and do manly things."

"I resent that! It's a perfectly good name."

"Oh? Why don't you ever use it then? All you use is the initial W, as if the name were some nasty little secret."

"How did we get started on this subject?"

"Because of all the junk in the hall."

"That isn't *junk*!"

"What do you call it?"

"I will try to explain. A deer is one of the cleverest creatures in the woods. He is the supreme test of a hunter's character and cunning, and it is useless to go after him half-prepared. So what you speak of as junk is in fact very highly specialized equipment. Camouflage clothing, face net , gloves, orange vest, waterproof boots, poncho, miniature flashlight, binoculars, maps, compass, hand-warmers, rifle, ammo, skinning knife and spray cans of doe scent."

"I thought it was bucks you're after."

"Right. The doe scent attracts them."

"Well, if you ask me," she said, "it looks like you're going to war."

"That's what it is. Mortal combat."

"And how long will you stay out there?"

"Until there's not a man or a deer standing."

"With all those fellows crowded into a little cabin, how do you keep your gear from getting mixed up?"

"We mark our stuff."

"It's like sending kiddies off to camp."

She bent to look at the pile.

"But this tag says 'Leatherstocking.' "

"Must be a mistake."

"So does this one! They all say *Leatherstocking*. I knew it!"

"I'm out of here," I told her. "I'll see you in a couple of weeks."

"Be careful," she said. "Don't shoot anybody's cows. And try to come back feeling better about yourself."

35

Ours is a dry camp. Not "dry" in the sense of a dry state. After guns are unloaded and the sun goes down, how hunters refresh themselves is their own business.

But with the hard weather coming early this fall, the cabin's fragile water system had to be shut off and drained. For city men used to certain amenities, the loss of plumbing is an awful blow. Water for drinking, cooking and washing dishes is not the issue. Enough for those purposes can be carried from town in plastic jugs.

Nor is bathing a particular concern. Creatures of the forest, with their keen scenting powers, are repelled by the odor of soap. After a few days away from home, hunters become creatures of the forest. They can detect the smell of the bacon and pancakes at the cafe on the courthouse square from a distance of 10 miles or more. But they no longer notice each other.

No, what saddens city hunters in a dry camp is

the errands they must occasionally make to the austere little edifice that stands among the trees out back of the plumbingless cabin.

As privies go, ours is a wonder - a palace, you might almost say. It even includes (and I neglected to mention this when describing it earlier) a braided carpet on the floor. But on a morning when the mercury has sunk away toward zero and put a layer of frost on the wooden seat, a visit to that facility can be an electrifying experience for gentlemen of delicate temperament.

They find no comfort in knowing that generations of their forefathers may have passed through life without even hearing of any different sort of sanitary accommodation. To speak of that is like alluding to a time before cell phones, before hot tubs, before credit cards and DVD players and even laptop computers – a time of unimaginable antiquity.

They only know that they have worked hard, achieved a certain standing in the world, have invested important sums in weapons, clothing and equipment. And now, having arrived for what they supposed would be a week of sport and civil fellowship, they are faced with THIS.

"Well, boys," I announce, "we are roughing it."

Their faces are long, their disappointment keen.

"At this very minute," I tell them, "there are millions of people in the Third World who would be glad to live as we are living."

But that is no consolation either. These are not Third World men. Some of them are men less than two hours by car from their homes – homes in which the taps give water on command, and the climate is regulated by thermostat, and frost on the seat is unknown. They are beginning to care a great deal less about whether they will see game in the forest. In fact, they are overcome by doubts about the whole enterprise. Especially doubtful, after a night of 10 degrees, are the hunters who elected to sleep in a tent.

The rest of us bunk in the cabin, warmed by the little wood stove. Some years the temperature is so mild a fire is not even required.

Several seasons ago, one member of our party began tenting out behind. He said it was on account of my snoring. In the mornings he would join us for coffee, and to use the plumbing before going to the woods. Sleeping out became an issue of principle. He was committed to it. This year he brought a friend who, whatever his wants in the matter, found himself locked into this business with the tent.

Now the weather has turned preternaturally cold, and there is not even the plumbing to look forward to in the morning. Only coffee, and that frosty seat.

Before many days I expect the atmosphere to turn sullen. Men will begin complaining of headaches and loss of appetite. They will remember things they have to do back in the city. One by one they will make their manners, as civilly as they can, and with the season not even half over will turn their cars back along the highway.

A dry camp is bad for regularity, but it is a blessing for the deer.

36

The old coyote came toward me through the brush and trees, casting to right and left, nose to the leaves, hunting a meal. Something was strange about the way he moved. Then I could see why.

His left front leg had been injured - in a trap, perhaps, or in an argument with a farm dog or another of his kind. He carried the leg up, putting no weight on it at all, and loped awkwardly on the other three. The margin for a wild hunter is a fine one. Disabled that way, it must have been hard for him to make a living. His condition looked poor.

The breeze was blowing from him to me up the timbered draw. I sat with the gun resting on my knee and watched for several minutes as he coursed through the trees and undergrowth. There was pain and a hungry urgency in his searching. Then I drew air between my lips to make a squeak – the distressed little cry a hurt rabbit makes. He stopped in midstride, as still as a gray statue at 50 yards down the draw. I squeaked again and could tell he had fixed the sound. He wasn't sure what had made it

– maybe a rabbit, or possibly or some kind of bird. But whatever it might be, its name was *dinner.*

He came on more cautiously now, putting a tree between himself and that sound. But I could watch him all the way as he came in. His coat was ragged, the bush of his tail a miserable, sparse appendage. There seemed hardly anything left of him but fur and bones, and the determination to try to make it through one more day.

I could let him go on about his rounds of pain. Or – and a case could be made for this – with the least movement of a finger I could end his hunger and his hurting. The gun was pointed directly at him as he came, and I had several moments to consider what was right. Then he stepped around the tree and into the clear.

The distance between us was 10 feet, or a dozen at most. We looked each other full in the face. I can't know what he made of me, except that I was a larger beast than he'd expected to find there. He halted, not so much in fear as in surprise at having been so fooled. The silver of his pointed muzzle ran back to the black mask from which two yellow eyes looked out. His ears were pricked forward, his face framed by a wolfish ruff.

If I'd seen in his expression anything of cowering or self-pity I might have done what it had occurred to me to do. But there was none of that. What shone from those eyes was only the unyielding, implacable will that drove him on. So the decision was made.

"Hello, coyote," I said.

He retreated a step and cocked his head sideways, doglike, to take my measure. I lifted one hand to be certain he clearly understood I wasn't for eating.

"Go on about your business," I told him. "You'll need some luck."

He did, limping off three-legged, then stopping just a few steps away to give me that cocked-head look again. *What are you?* his expression seemed to ask. *And why are you here?*

Reasonable questions, those. And if I don't know the certain answers, there's no reason to think he

would. I've never felt a closer communion with any
creature in the wild. Then he stepped deliberately
behind a little bush, and like a shadow of something
only imagined he was gone.

37

This year's deer hunt has been different than
the failed chases of the past. This year I have seen
game.

First I saw that coyote. Now I've seen a skunk.

We met in the dark hour of morning as I made
my way along a pasture's edge toward the wooded
draw I planned to hunt. The skunk had been drinking at a puddle in the path, and looked up surprised
into my flashlight's beam. Then he trotted ahead of
me, as companionable as a pointer pup – but with
his tail in the vertical position – all the way to my
deer stand.

I didn't molest him. In 30-some years of hunting I have taken care never to go up against any

creature able to shoot back. And, notwithstanding the evident good nature of this one, skunks do shoot back.

The morning was frosty – the adjective country people use when they mean to say subarctic. My hands lost all sensation. My face shriveled like a fig. An urgent rustling filled the pallid dawn. It was, I discovered, the sound of me shaking inside my coat. The skunk, repelled by the spectacle of such discomfort, went on about his errands in the forest and left me frozen against my tree.

Squirrels appeared from their leaf nests. An owl passed by. A legion of redheaded woodpeckers set up a drumming overhead. The squirrels presented fleeting targets. The woodpeckers were too far away. And I would not eat owl even if it were legal, which it is not. From a great distance there rose the reports of heavy armament. Every year, in the first hour of the season's opening, one hears that cannonade.

It is meaningless. All across the wooded hills disappointed men are shooting off their rifles to stay warm. But they soon tired of that and the racket subsided. The sun surmounted the trees and the day slightly warmed. I found a cookie in my pocket and ate it. Then returned to my duty, guarding the forest – or that part of it I could see – against the accidental intrusion of any deer.

No deer came. And no more skunks.

I met two of my friends in the appointed meadow, and we walked together to the car. On the road, men passed in pickup trucks carrying deer they'd had shipped in, already slain and dressed, in refrigerator vans from other states. Those men meant to give the impression they'd shot the deer that morning in woods neighboring my own. But my friends and I were not born yesterday. We know a deerless forest when we see one. And each year we see one.

The cabin stove had burned low. Even so, it was finer there than leaning against a tree. We made breakfast. Venison sausage – a gift of the season before, from one of those importers of western deer. Three eggs apiece. Biscuits and gravy. Baked beans, left over from the night before. Orange juice. Coffee and sweet rolls, heated on the stove. And after that we slept.

That is the supreme moment of a deer hunt – late in the morning of the opening day, when you have gotten your limit at the breakfast table and can sleep a lazy hour or two before going out again to look for skunks and woodpeckers. Sleeping, I dreamed of owl meat. I dreamed of going home with an owl tied to the fender of the car and having a few people in for supper to celebrate the success of the hunt.

Outside, on the road in front of the cabin, men in red hats in jeeps could be heard driving slowly along the blacktop. They were road hunting, looking for any deer that might have fallen out of the refrigerator vans and rolled into the ditches. The stove creaked with warming. A wasp, roused from its winter torpor, hummed lazily in the rafters. The biscuits lay heavy on our hearts.

We love this yearly outing, my friends and I. We do not hunt to impress wives with our manliness or our skill as providers. Or to cut a figure at the country general store, sitting around on pop cases and regaling other hunters with stories of great bucks dropped on the run at 600 yards. No, the attraction of the sporting life is, for us, more basic and more practical. We hunt to eat.

And, as you can see, we do eat. Very well.

38

The deer season draws toward its end. Being already identified as a hunter, I can proceed directly to speak about this without the customary prior confessions of depravity. Ours has been a splendid outing, rich in memories. The dominant memory is of forgetting to take an alarm clock, an oversight which required me to jerk upright in a panic every half-hour or so through the night and read my watch dial by match light, ensuring that my guests would not be tardy for their appointments with the dawn.

The days have fallen into a pattern. We wake in the cold cabin, stir the wood stove to life, and dress in many layers of clothes, then give our attention to what I like to think of as a pre-breakfast of sweet rolls and leftover beans. The real breakfast, which I have described already, comes later. But this early snack arms us against any possibility of future disappointment.

Then we go forth to our designated stations in the forest to become as much a part of nature as squirrels and birds. This merging with nature begins at the point where haunch meets stone or damp earth and spreads outward through insulated socks and space-age underwear. Thoughts of deer are replaced by contemplation of one's own immediate pain and a determination never to spend another autumn morning as a squirrel or a woodpecker.

Then, mercifully, it gets to be daylight.

Except for the hour of rising, there are not many electric moments in deer hunting. I did hear a deer approach – late the second afternoon, I think it was. Its tiny hooves made a hesitant crunching sound in the oak leaves. Nearer it came, while I waited beside my tree. Finally the beast stepped out into a little clearing standing broadside at a range of no more than 20 yards, still unaware of me there, still entirely unalarmed.

The only trouble is that it wasn't a deer. It was a rotund trespasser with pink cheeks and a $500 orange leather hunting suit and some sort of outlandish 2-foot-long pistol in a holster strapped to his middle. The exchange that followed was short and not so cordial. He allowed as how he might be lost. I agreed that seemed to be the case, and directed him to my nearest fence.

That was my one worthwhile shot of the season and, right or wrong, I passed it up.

39

It was a day of boyhood, lived as a gift in middle age.

Outside the cabin, a fine new snow – unmarked by any footstep – lay away through the sparkling filigree of woods. The morning was fresh, not really cold. And soon, in the west, the hem of the last night's storm drew up to show a sky of palest, farthest blue.

A snow changes the land. Clefts and valleys become less definite. Rivulets vanish under the layering of white. I struck out walking, well-booted against the wet. And after 20 minutes, when I'd

passed the same known place three times and had
crossed and re-crossed my own meandering foot-
prints, it was clear that I was lost.

Lost in a little piece of woods I know as famil-
iarly as I know my city yard, on a walk I have taken
in nearly every weather for more than half my
life! But I know the perimeter of that bit of forest,
bounded on three sides by wires and on the fourth
by a road. So there was no terror in the wandering.
In fact, it was a pleasure just to stride on, and to see
the land as if for the first time, through the eyes of
some disoriented stranger passing that way.

For most of two hours I walked in the footsteps
of a deer. A smallish doe, she must have been, from
the look of the prints. Unalarmed, she proceeded at
her own rate, pausing sometimes to paw the snow
aside and nip a bit of woodland grass. Her meander-
ings were wonderfully intricate, the delicate path
she made bending many times back upon itself.
And though not frightened, it was plain she knew
that I – or something – was following her.

More than once I could see where she'd put the
mark of her hoof directly in my own fresh boot

track. Another time, on a stone outcrop at the head of a little valley, I found where she had stood behind a screen of leaves to watch the graceless thing in a coat plod slowly by below. Finally, tiring of the game, she turned in several quick circles. And from the last of those no track at all emerged. She simply vanished without trace in the empty morning, as a thought can do in an inattentive instant.

I sat to rest, then, on a log on the valley's side, where a small stream cutting darkly through the whiteness dropped over a ledge of rock with a happy splash. Squirrels came out on their branches to object. Two red ones and a gray. Maybe I was sitting where they'd buried nuts against just such a snowy emergency. For whatever reason, they wanted me out of there. One of them, deliberately, I think, loosed a shower of wet snow from the limb above directly down the collar of my coat.

From somewhere in the far north and east, a high, thin piping could be heard. Then louder, nearer. It was the cry of wild geese in flight – whose music lifts the heart from autumn through spring.

What resting place they'd been dislodged from

by the past night's weather I couldn't know. But they were on the move, driving with collective purpose down the long slant of the season. First a single ragged skein of them, a family group. Then more and larger formations. Until all the air, as far as could be seen in any direction above the valley, was full of them – the V's breaking off and drifting a bit apart, then recombining with the main wave.

They never stopped passing. Or I listening. Then I climbed up through the trees to a small field, in which blackbirds – many thousand of them – rose up with the sound of a shaken blanket and coiled like an enormous smoke cloud, then settled back again when I'd gone on.

It's all there is to tell. Just small things. It was a day when you'd almost think you might walk forever, on legs that never tired. With a piece of cold rabbit and a biscuit in the pocket of your coat, you could wander lost like that for hours, not even caring to find your way until the woods started to turn blue, and dark was coming on.

That is how it used to be, I thought – and for the shortest moment almost could remember.

Then, hopelessly found again, I struck back on a straight line to where I'd started. And closed the cabin for the winter – unplugged the refrigerator, switched on the mouser, snapped the lock on the door – and drove the long road home.

Winter

40

After several gentler previews, the bitter season has arrived in earnest. On a recent afternoon I drove through failing light to the cabin at the wood's edge. That place is important to me in every season, but it was the time I'd spent alone there in the dark of a long-ago year that had determined, in some way, the shape of my life since.

I wanted to see how much of it memory had saved, how much had been lost.

Even with twilight coming, the distant buzz of wood saws still could be heard across the timbered hills. In that country, where comfort is an iron stove fed with oak and hickory chunks, people take their woodpiles seriously. Seeing some dooryard where the winter's supply is neatly corded up, you know it's a place lived in by thrifty and provident folk. If only a few sticks are strewn carelessly beside the porch, you can be sure the inhabitants there are doomed by fecklessness.

Winter separates the doers from the dawdlers in an unforgiving way.

One-third of nearly every day in that distant winter of my youth I spent cutting and carrying firewood. At first I had only a hand saw, an ax, two steel wedges. And I worked by myself, staying inside when the wind blew hard, knowing that if a tree fell wrong I'd be caught with no one to call out to for help.

Then a wiry little man in his 70s arrived from somewhere in Oklahoma, to put his wreck of a house trailer in the woods across the gravel lane. And after that he and I cut wood together. Ed Mongold was his name. He had a power saw that he'd cobbled together from parts he'd found at a sale somewhere – a mad contraption with a monstrous circular blade, as big around as a barrel lid, driven by a lawn mower engine and a fantastic tangle of pulleys and belts, all this mounted on two treadless car tires. OSHA would not have approved, but of course there was no OSHA then.

Some mornings the old engine refused to start. Or the main drive belt would loosen and come off.

Once the saw blade itself, lethal as a guillotine, spun free and sailed away several feet to lodge in a standing tree. But that saw of his, when it was working, could chew through a 2-foot log in less time than it takes to tell it. And he and I became, according to the size of our wood stacks, two of the provident ones.

However cold the morning was, we'd warm to our work. For an occasional break, we'd upend a couple of chunks and sit on them, coats open, get out our cans of Prince Albert and rolling papers, and make ourselves a couple of smokes, contented as only men can be when they're sure of having wood enough to get them through to a kinder season.

He intended to make a humble but lasting home in that stretch of country. Being young, I had a grander and more foolish notion of writing something that would get me fame and a lot of money. That's not how it worked out for either of us. His wife died, and he drifted off to someplace else. I went back to the city and took regular employment.

Nearly 50 years have passed since then, and when I came almost at dark the other evening, my woodpile was a scandal – a few half-rotten chunks nearly hidden under drifts of leaves. I kindled a fire and started the cabin warming. From the edge of the clearing out behind, an owl boomed – a descendant, perhaps, of the one who lived there when I did. In that moment, I almost could believe that no time had passed and nothing had changed. I was young again, and the little man from across the road might any minute knock at the door to sit and smoke and tell a story.

The night was cloudy, with no moon or stars. I lay down in the lightless room. My fire of punky wood shifted and settled, and the old stove creaked as it began to cool. I could feel the remembered loneliness coming, even before sleep did. And I woke at first daybreak as cold as I can recall ever being.

The man isn't the boy, I thought, and the past can't be lived again. Better to let recollection shape and soften what really was. Fingers trembling so I hardly could fasten the buttons of my coat, I shut the door and hurried away from there – eager for the city house where tame cats and a tame man can sit together before the hearth and count their luck.

41

There's always some new danger, isn't there? If it isn't killer bees or Lyme disease, then it's killer hamburgers or Mexican tomatoes. Now comes this alarm about the mouse disease, a virus first identified in the American southwest and believed to be advancing relentlessly eastward.

Most of the warnings I ignore. But the mouse virus has a serious sound to it. So on a bright winter day I decided to make a run to the cabin to be sure the electronic mouse repeller was doing its job. Mice used to be a major problem. I've never seen an intelligence report on the enemy's strength, but its safe to say the number of them in that country neighborhood must be stupendous. No matter how many casualties they suffer, they can just keep sending fresh troops at you.

The anti-mouse device is mounted on the inside wall above the door and emits a shrill screech that mice and other pests seem unable to bear. It has been quite effective. But as I entered the screened porch and approached the door I did not hear the distinctive sound. And found, when I went inside, that evidently on some past visit I'd forgotten to plug the thing in before leaving, and I'd paid a price for that carelessness.

There were mouse droppings on a shelf and in two drawers of a cabinet, and pieces had been chewed out of a pillow case. The predations, though minor, were annoying. Clearly I had lodgers. So with the truce broken, I put out poison baits under the cabinet and put traps behind the couch. Then I set the mouser screeching and left the chemicals and wicked little machines to do their work.

A couple of weeks later, another errand took me in the direction of the cabin, so I made a brief stop to see how the campaign was going. What I found did not make me proud.

Of the four traps, one was unsprung, one sprung but empty. The other two had snapped shut with deadly effect. I carried the corpses out and deposited them in the winter leaf-litter at the edge of the woods. Two more casualties were in an empty wastebasket. Those went out, too, although with the cabin's primitive water system shut down for winter, the sterilizing of the container will have to wait for a warmer season.

Four dead. No wounded. Even as I was disposing of them, I could not help thinking how many hundred others, more likely thousands, were watching, listening, waiting to come in. Like a general sickened by the day's spectacle, I decided then to go down the lane behind the cabin to spend a little quiet time away from the carnage, contemplating the frozen pond and the spare winter woodland.

My walking shoes were beside a chair in the back room. There used to be scorpions in that country – small, with a sting like a wasp's, painful but not dangerous. What's become of them I can't say. They've just disappeared. But, governed by old habit, I shook the shoes before putting them on. Out fell a mouse, dead as a stone, and also his little cache of blue granules – the poison he'd carried in there with him, imagining it would get him through to spring.

Somehow after that I didn't feel so much like walking. What I wanted was just to be out and away from there, and get on about my errand in the town.

Nevertheless before leaving, just to be safe, I reset my traps and put out fresh containers of the lethal bait. Once the battle's joined, I suppose the only thing's to see it through to the end.

And what might that end be? It's not even in doubt. They have the place surrounded. A generation of them born today can replicate itself two or three times more before the willows green. I'm large and they are small, and technology is on my side. But time and my carelessness are on theirs. If their virus doesn't get me, it's sure their patience will.

What use are body counts in a war that can't be won?

42

An unseasonable spell of dry and windy days has parched the land. And like the viper that comes out to sun on a stone, that low form of country life – the arsonist – has begun to stir again.

Wildfire is the terror of my Ozark neighborhood two seasons of the year, in late winter or early spring before the greening, and again in autumn when the oak leaves fall and every woodlot is a tinder box. Some of the burning plainly is malicious, but more – probably most – is the work of accidental foolishness. The day is comfortable for being outdoors. The hours stretch emptily ahead. One way or other, time must be made to pass. So some citizen takes it in his head to burn a bit of brush.

If you asked him why, the reason he might give is that it will kill the ticks. Or make way for grass to grow. Or simply "clean things up a little." Logic is powerless against these notions. Burning neither discourages the tick, a hardy brute, nor transforms woodland into pasture. But the myths are as old as the people's habitation of those hills, and are transmitted from one generation to the next with the authority of fact.

Generally, I believe, no deliberate harm is meant. The burner intends to contain the fire on his own property. Never mind that the humidity is low and a gusting breeze has risen. Or that he's setting about the task without help or tools. The thing to do is strike the match, and then see how events unfold. It isn't spite, exactly. It's something sadder and more dangerous than that.

Three years ago, fire came across the road into my field and took several hundred dollars' worth of hay bales and a half-mile of fence. Last year it burned a corner of my woods and started into the field again, before the volunteer fire department arrived from 15 miles away to put it out. Afterward, these events take on an aura of the miraculous, like weeping marble statues or faces of prophets seen in the clouds.

People tell of strange pickup trucks seen passing slowly on the road. Or of finding suspicious cans that may have contained gasoline. Or there are rumors, told thirdhand, of a threat made by someone with an imagined grudge. It comes to nothing. Ever. Fire is accepted as a kind of cosmic magic, no more to be understood or resisted than birth, death or the workings of government.

I had a call one recent day from a man whose house is just down the road from my wooded corner.

"It's that time of year," he said. "I guess you know what's happening."

"Fire?"

"It's coming through the woods about 300 feet from your cabin, burning fast. We're trying to stop it, but the wind's bad. The fire department's on the way."

I raced two hours down the highway, stomach knotted, and got there just at nightfall. Hollow trees stood burning like candles where the fire had passed. But the wind had shifted a bit to eastward. The volunteer firemen had gotten there in time. The things I cared most about were spared.

Best of all, I got to know my new neighbor. He was still there, tired and ash-dusted after his labors on my behalf. A young man with a young family, he's a transplant from another state. He brought with him a deep concern for nature and a hatred for wildfires that's as implacable as mine. We stood together in the gathering dark, and I had a consoling thought. It takes a while – may take years, or even generations. But one day, that man and I, or our children, or our children's children, will have the burners outnumbered.

Time will burn them, as surely as they've burned the land.

43

On a different day, one uncommonly warm for February, an errand took me to a town not far from the farm. My business there was brief, so when I'd finished I made a small detour to the cabin, just to prowl a bit for the pure pleasure of it. Showers were forecast, but hadn't yet begun. All the countryside – fields and forest – lay serene in the sleep of the year. In the deep of winter you rarely get a day so sweet.

I set out without a fixed destination, always the finest way to travel, letting impulse show the way.

Ice had retreated two feet or more from the margins of the cabin pond. On the far side, at the woods' edge, a band of whitetail deer – eight of them, at least, and maybe more unseen in the shadow – lifted their heads, barked sharply and were gone. Passing crows broadcast the news of a walker spied below. Coarse-voiced woodpeckers fled away among the trees.

I noticed for the first time the green of young pine trees pushing up through the leaf litter, a new generation of them seeded out from the ones my wife and I planted those many springs ago. The ones that were trapped and stunted by the shade of the oaks, still are spindly things, scarcely more than head high after all this time. But the ones that found the light have shot up to make a towering presence against the sky.

In every soft place could be found the signs of creatures who use the land more regularly than I: hoof impressions and bark-rubbings left by the deer, hand prints of raccoons, mounds of hickory shells and acorn fragments directly below the den trees of the squirrels. Passing slowly, bound for no appointments, you notice all these things.

A streamlet running down from the upper meadow to feed the pond spills over a lichen-crusted outcropping and makes a little pool that in sum-

mer is populous with frogs. It's a place where my
mother liked to come. I stopped a moment there,
then stepped across and went on up to the meadow
itself, its cover of native grasses russet-colored in
this season. Suddenly a memory came clear.

On a December day – it must have been 20 years
ago – I stepped into that little field behind a dog
on point, and out of the waist-high cover the quail
burst up like a flock of blackbirds. I don't know
how many there were. At least 150, or maybe more.
Several coveys of them had for some reason come
together in that one place, and they just kept exploding from the grass in waves. It's a thing I've never
seen before or since. We stood there smitten by
wonder, the dog and I, and I never even raised the
gun.

Everywhere on that land I'm in the company of
shadows – of memories from which the joy or the
grief is not quite gone.

Coolness had come into the afternoon, and the
pale sun had declined to just above the west woodline. As they invariably do, my steps had taken me
in a long circle past the tree house built for little

girls grown now to women, then down to the pond again. And always I can find my parents there – just their shadows, but no less real presences for that. My father is hacking back weeds and brush with his machete from the water's edge. My mother is in the boat by herself, and I hear her little cry of happiness as another fish pulls the bobber under.

It's not my nature or my wish to live endlessly in the past, but it is reassuring, when the spirit's inclined, to know a place where those good memories can come so alive again.

A pair of mallards burst up suddenly out of dry cattails across the pond, and I was drawn back into the present moment. Were those ducks all-year residents, or had the spell of mild weather called them back early to seek somewhere for nesting?

I'd seen how the tree buds already had begun swelling in anticipation of a spring still likely several snows and many freezes away. And expectant as those trees, I was able to imagine the fields greening, birdfoot violets showing in the new grass, toads singing, quail whistling and delicate ferns uncurling their fronds in the valley.

In six more weeks, maybe sooner, the wild gobblers would be greeting dawn's first pale light from their branches on the hillside just above. A month after that there'd be morel mushrooms pushing up, dogwoods in bloom and heavy bass will be thrashing hungrily in the shallows.

All of that I was imagining as I went up the lane from the pond back to the cabin. An excursion that has taken only minutes to tell here occupied the better part of two hours.

Such an afternoon had begun to wash me clean of winter and let me sense the year dependably advancing. Spring might seem very distant still. But less distant than yesterday. And tomorrow would come as it always does – all in a breathless rush.

44

Sitting on the cabin porch, I can hear across a distance of nearly a mile the growl of machines at work, completing the earthen dam of what will be the lake of my longtime dreaming.

A tree-house built for two small girls.
– Charles Porter photo

Gray fox kits venture from their den.

Their littermates come out to explore.

Cold-weather plumbing.
– Charles Porter photo

Crimson daybreak over promising water.
- Chris Peditto photo

After years of dreaming, the new lake – a splendid fishery.
- Gary Carter photo

Anne's big bluegill is a typical catch.

Jennie with a late-summer trophy bass.

October reflections: Charles in an earlier year.
- Jack Jonathan photo

C. Wesley Leatherstocking, looking like a leaf.
– Charles Porter photo

Two autumns ago we did our survey in the
Y-shaped valley and the contractor, Tom Williams,
placed his flagged stakes marking what will be the
eventual shoreline. Then a timber cutter harvested
the marketable trees from the basin, including the
majestic walnut that had delayed for many years my
going forward with this project I'd so long imagined.

Construction was begun that December, then
halted by wet winter weather and resumed again
last spring. The lake will be 35 feet deep at the dam,
but will have two arms, shallower at their upper
ends, to provide ideal areas for the fish to spawn.
While work was in progress, a 12-inch pipe was
installed at the dam's base to keep the basin dry.

Then, on an early spring night, there was a near
calamity. An evening storm rolled in and dumped
a torrential rain. Tom Williams sprang from his bed,
rushed to the work site and, in pitch darkness, managed to get his valuable machines – two bulldozers
and a scraper – to high ground just in time. The
torrent of runoff into the valley had driven a log
like a well-aimed arrow directly into the drain pipe,
blocking the outlet and causing the basin to begin

to fill. By morning, water was 15 feet deep at the dam. A large diesel pump had to be brought from the city and run for nine consecutive days and nights until the basin was emptied, the blocked drain could be opened and, when the site dried, work could commence again.

Our expectation is that construction will be finished this coming autumn. And by next spring the lake will have begun to fill. In anticipation of that, we've already begun planting trees.

Two scarlet maples went on a high point that, when surrounded by water, will be a small island. The rest – not actually trees but nuts, which represent the possibility of trees – we distributed among the oaks on the hillsides rising from what will be the shore: a hundred or more black walnuts, gathered in our city yard; nearly that many horse chestnuts collected last year under the grand old trees of Madrid's Retiro Park. It wasn't as much work as it sounds. In that kind of planting, all you have to do is spade open a slit 2 or 3 inches deep, drop in the nut and press the earth closed over it with your shoe. After that you hope.

"The squirrels will get some of them," a forester cautioned. "But they won't get them all." By some time in early summer we should know how many of the nuts have sprouted. And next year we hope to put in 300 seedlings of shortleaf pine and 50 of deciduous holly. These additions, if they take, will add variety to the largely oak and hickory forest.

And I can imagine the valley as it will one day surely be. In spring, the white candles of the horse chestnut blossoms will shine brightly among the darker foliage of the oaks. The slender trunks of mature pines will reflect handsomely in a lake surface stirred to ripples by rising fish. The maples on the island and the holly trees on the facing bank will have grown tall and full, and with the turn to autumn they will come wonderfully aflame. An army of squirrels, at work in a rain of yellow walnut leaves, will be hurrying to gather and store up nuts to see them through the harder season.

All of that I can see with perfect clarity in my mind's eye – as surely as our daughters and their children will one day see it in actual truth in their own time. And I find that immensely satisfying, even if I will not be witness to the maturing.

There's something of immortality in the act of planting trees. It may not be quite the sort of after-life some people hope for. But it's reward enough for me.

45

On a March day, when the south wind was sweet with an early promise of spring, a friend and I spent several hours cutting trail. Actually, we were re-opening a lane some other man, or men, had made through the woodland long ago. How long? Three generations before us, maybe more.

I'd known the old trace was there – had come across it once or twice before. A wagon road, it must have been. Or possibly a post road, bringing letters from the outer world to the folk who'd settled in the vastness of that piece of Ozark forest. But a century of leaf falls and limb falls had buried and blocked it. Unless you were looking, you might not notice it at all.

It took us the better part of an hour to find it again

and determine, exactly, its route. Then we set to
work with ax and saws, clearing away the deadfalls
and hacking back the brush. Sometimes the old
road passed across a stony shelf, or through an area
where great oaks cast their shade and the undergrowth was sparse. There we made fast leaps ahead.
In other places the gain of a few yards cost half an
hour. The destination, we knew at the start, was an
upland glade three-quarters of a mile ahead.

Two families, at least, had once lived there. You
still can find the foundation stones of their cabins,
though the cabins themselves are vanished, gone
to fire or rot. From the arrangement of the stones
you can count the rooms – two in one dwelling,
three in the other. The meadows in linked series
along the ridge top, grown up now in sprouts and
berry thickets, would have been the poor fields from
which those people tried to wring a crop. The small
creek flowing below would have been their source
of household water.

How desperately hard must their lives have been!

The soil is poor, shallowly underlain by stone.
The only work, if it could be found, would have

been hacking railroad ties at a nickel apiece. And once the homestead clearings had been made, man and mule would have had no rest from holding the relentless forest back and keeping it from claiming everything again.

That's the place our road was leading to. From there it would descend a ledged hillside and continue on along what has been a farming track in continuous use, across two larger, newer fields, then ford a stream and come out finally onto what now is a paved county highway. As we worked, from early morning on to noon and past, I could not stop thinking of the people whose cabins had fronted on this rough lane. Were they lonely there in the deepness of the woods? How often had they traveled out to spend part of a day or night in some place where other voices could be heard?

Did they know – or even suspect – how futile was their endless, profitless toil? Could they imagine ahead to a time when their houses would be gone, their fields returned to sprouty meadows again and their road unfindable? I doubt it. Like most of us, I suppose, they believed their lives had some lasting purpose.

In middle afternoon, we finished cutting. We had reached the last clearing. The way behind us lay open, fit for a buggy or even a car to travel. Our palms were raw and our backs sore, but the result was wonderfully satisfying. "We've done it!" we cried out to one another proudly, and shook hands on it. But in that moment, some part of my mind stood a bit apart, considering those foundation stones, those ruined fields.

Temporary, it was whispering. You know it – or you know nothing at all.

46

As this winter nears its end, there's been one late snow – probably the last. It has caused me to reflect again on that season of cold and stillness I spent here in this cabin when I was in my 20s, alone and aimless, still undecided about what work I cared to do.

The lady in the farmhouse a half-mile up the road kept hens and sold the eggs for a penny each. Flour and salt and powdered milk, apples, onions and other provisions could be gotten at a little country store, four miles away by foot. In the timber were squirrels and rabbits in dependable supply. Stove wood was plentiful. Rationed out carefully, one good-sized bottle of spirits lasted the winter through. My expenses averaged just over $4 a month, and I lacked nothing, really. I'd have lived comfortably enough, had it not been for those bitter nights. Probably there've been worse ones since, but none I remember quite so vividly.

For stretches of whole weeks the daytime temperatures never got above the teens. At night, the mercury in the thermometer on an outside wall sank away to 7 degrees below zero, sometimes to 10 below. Always, in a small, dark hour, the fire in my drafty stove would burn away to ash. The cold would come seeping through my sleeping bag. And by morning there would be a skim of ice on the water bucket.

That was only creature discomfort, though, and bearable enough. Worse by far was the lack of any sort of companionship. I had no neighbors, really. And friends from the city only rarely came to visit. Days would pass without my hearing a word spoken. Then those two stray beagle pups joined me, and my situation greatly improved. They slept warm on my feet at night, and were good company in the woods, or on the floor beside the table where I worked at trying to be a writer.

Then the season turned. Spring peepers sang from the creek below the pond, and violets bloomed. I was awakened in the night not by cold but by the cries of geese returning northward.

The spareness of my lifestyle had reduced the need for money almost to nothing. I remember thinking that if I somehow managed to sell even one story, it would buy another year there. Maybe I'd have been there still. Except that every story I sent off to editors came back rejected, sometimes without even a note. Things did not work out as I'd imagined.

It was necessary, then, to find a regular job. So I came back to the city. And took up this work that has given me such satisfaction. And met the woman who's shared with me the laughter and struggles and joys that our years together have contained, and who bore the two daughters who are our pride and great happiness.

Curious, isn't it, the odd turns a life can take? Looking back now, it's clear that every important piece of luck I've had – everything I care most about in this world – I owe to having failed.

AN AFTERWORD

Dorothy caught a great fish from the pond. Hugh retired. One evening he stood holding his smallest granddaughter under the weight of near stars and told her – he who never rode an airplane – that there were men walking on the moon. Another afternoon he raked up leaves in a pile for the girls to jump in. The next day he died; Dorothy the next year. And now the girls are grown and gone.

That's the standard chronology of lives, isn't it? Ordinary losses. In the usual order.

Now, through the long dark of every year, the cabin mostly is untenanted. For a weekend in November, several friends and I use it as a base for scouting out legendary breakfasts in country cafes, while speaking in the abstract of hunting deer. Then I snap the padlock shut, we drive out the gate, the iron stove creaks away to cold, and winter closes down.

But during the frozen months, when I am a

prisoner of ambition and city walls, my mind goes often to that little woods cabin. And foolish as the notion is, I wonder sometimes if a floor can miss footsteps, if old boards can miss the sounds of being lived between.

Not that the desertion is quite complete. The survivor mice still occasionally harbor there, safe from gunfire. They materialize with the frost, coming from somewhere – from under leaves, from out of their tunnels in the bent grass – to find a surer shelter. Somewhere between the foundation stones they find a crevice. Or where two boards do not perfectly join a crack is enlarged by an eternity of patient gnawing.

Oh, there are means of killing once they're in – poisons, traps. And the newfangled noise maker discourages them. But what, really, is the point. The actual damage they do is much exaggerated. A part of a page of newspaper – not enough to start a stove fire, and bearing only antique news about the world, if any news at all – may be shredded to make a provident nest. Tinned and bottled food is safe enough. It's true a bar of soap may be eaten. But, heaven knows, if hunger comes to that they're welcome to it. Then, in spring, after ice has left the pond but before the violets or the first peeping of frogs, the mice are gone again.

Recently I made the two-hour drive to open the cabin for another year, as I have done – or helped to do – for all but one of the last 50 Aprils. This time I went alone. The stove, my old iron friend, came willingly alight to chase the last memory of chill. The coffee water warmed. There was no sense at all of any interruption. I was struck, as I always am, by how easily and naturally life returns to a house so long neglected and how soon the abandonment is forgotten. More than that, I could not help marveling at the power of so humble and small a place to guard such a store of private history, keeping all of it safe, unchanged, through the seasons and the years.

As I sat with the hot cup, I could see at the room's far end a ceiling panel pieced clumsily together where Hugh cut it in error. And I could hear again, alive as anything, his cry of dismay on discovering he'd measured wrong. Outside, the redbuds were showing color, as they have every spring since I was young. Beside the porch was the quince a friend and I transplanted from beside the ruins of a fallen settler house. A few steps beyond was the flowering crab, a gift one year to my mother. She would have loved to see how splendid it has become. The pine trees at the edge of our clearing that a girl and I planted together – set out as switches on a bitter day a month before we married – have lengthened into solid presences against the sky.

Spring sunlight through the window struck to life the pictures on the walls. Some of them were photographs of people dead, of friends lost, smiling in beautiful indifference to rushing time. Others were drawings done in a childish hand by daughters who have gotten on with the adventures of their own lives. But there was no sadness in any of that. The cabin is like a time capsule. Much of what I have cared most about in the world is contained there – changeless. No matter how the years careen ahead, and no matter how long I am away, I can turn the key in the lock, step through the door, and it all resumes again. And that is reassuring, because the heart is prodigal. Eventually, unless you're careful, so much just gets away.

A single wasp, the last waker, circled against the

ceiling, dinged once against the metal light shade, then hummed benignly past my head and through the open door into the brilliance of the gentler season. The wasps, the mice, and me and all of mine, I was thinking then, are carried on the same quick flow. But what luck it is to have one place in the world where you know, whatever overtakes you, if only you can make it there once more, you have it all.